Neighbours

Sisters in the City

funtastic

funtastic™

First published in Australia by Funtastic Limited, 2005

800 Wellington Road, Rowville
Victoria 3178, Australia
Ph: 61 3 9213 0100 Fax: 61 3 9213 0199
www.funtastic.com.au
Email: publishing@funtastic.com.au

www.fremantlemedia.com

Thanks to Jon Fowler and Rachel Stevens.
Holly Valance's proceeds going to the Arthritis Foundation.

Written by Sarah Mayberry
Cover Illustration by Samantha Hollister
Designed by David Ciro
Printed and bound in Australia

10 9 8 7 6 5 4 3 2 1

Mayberry, Sarah, 1970- .
Neighbours : sisters in the city.

ISBN 1 74150 850 9.

1. Neighbours (Television program). 2. Romance fiction. I. Title.

A823.4

Neighbours

Sisters in the City

Sarah Mayberry

funtastic

Chapter 1

*F*lick was just smoothing conditioner into her hair when the soothing warmth of the shower abruptly cut to icy cold. Her body curled in a vain attempt to avoid the punishing spray, and she threw her head back and screamed a plea from the heart:

'Micheeelllleeee!!!'

A faint 'sorry' echoed through from the kitchen, and suddenly the hot water was back. Flick sighed and concentrated on rinsing the conditioner out of her long blonde hair. Clearly, living with her younger sister Michelle was going to present some challenges. First, there was the fact that her apartment only had one bedroom, and the living area was roughly equivalent to a shoebox. Then there was the mess factor. Michelle might be the brains of the family, but she was a pig in the tidy stakes. And then there was the all-important borrowing-of-clothes dynamic. She'd be kidding herself if she thought Michelle was suddenly going to start respecting her privacy and keep her mitts off her wardrobe just because they were in another country.

Despite all the apparent negatives, Flick smiled into the shower spray. It would be great living with Michelle. Although she'd never admit it aloud, she'd been lonely here in her poky, little apartment. She and Michelle had seen each other most weekends since her younger sister came to the US to study a year or so ago, but Flick still felt a certain hollowness when she trudged up the four flights of stairs to her apartment at the end of each day. It would be good to be the Scully girls again, to argue over who drank the last of the milk and what they were going to watch on TV.

Switching the water off, Flick pushed the shower curtain aside and reached for her towel. She mopped at her dripping wet hair, roughly towelled her body dry, and braced herself for the day's most demanding task—climbing out of the shower. It was actually a shower-over-bath, and the bath was a big, old claw-foot number that had looked incredibly inviting when Flick first saw the apartment. Add that to the fact that the apartment was rent controlled, in a reasonable part of town, and within a few subway stops of work, Flick had known a bargain when she saw one.

Then she'd had her first shower, and realised climbing out of the wet and slippery high-sided tub afterwards was a near-death experience. Just one of the many worms she'd discovered in her first few bites of the Big Apple.

Bracing her hands on the curled edge of the bath, Flick eased a leg over the side and felt around with her foot for the wooden stool she'd bought in an attempt to make the bath user-friendly. Foot firmly placed, she swung her other leg over, and finally stepped down to the ground.

'Degree of difficulty: nine point two,' she muttered under her breath as she padded back through to her bedroom.

'Hey, sorry about the water. I was making tea,' Michelle said as Flick passed through the living room.

Flick shook her head when she saw that Michelle was perched on the fold-out sofa bed eating toast in her pyjamas.

'Don't complain to me when your bed feels like sandpaper,' she warned.

'I won't, don't worry. What time will you be home from work?'

In her bedroom, Flick gave her hair one last vigorous rub and tried to remember her work timetable.

'I think normal time. No late shifts tonight.'

Crossing to the art deco chest of drawers she'd bought at a flea market, Flick rummaged around for some underwear. Pulling on knickers and a bra, she reached for the neatly pressed uniform shirt she'd hung at the ready the night before.

'You're so lucky. I wish I had your body.'

Flick turned to find Michelle slouched in the doorway, still munching on toast.

'Yeah, well I wish I had your boobs. Can't have everything, Shelly,' she said philosophically.

'I bet you eat whatever, right, and never put on weight?' Michelle asked enviously.

Flick shrugged a shoulder. 'Mum said she was like this when she was young, too. But once I hit thirty—bang, instant blimp if I don't watch it.'

Michelle sighed heavily. 'Why did I have to inherit from Dad's side of the family?'

'It could be worse, Shelly. You could have inherited the Aunt Valda gene,' Flick teased, referring to the woman who was actually their grandmother. Crazy, eccentric, out-there—call it what you will—Aunt Valda was a whole bowlful of weird.

Michelle shuddered comically and mooched her way back to the couch. Flick pulled on the black stockings, neat black skirt, and deep maroon blazer that made up the rest of the Lassiter's Towers Hotel uniform. 'It's true,' she thought as she checked her appearance in the mirror inside her wardrobe door. 'I am pretty lucky I'm tall and slim. Although, I'm never going to take out anyone's eye in the cleavage department.' Experimenting, Flick pushed up her boobs and checked the effect. Wrong. Like it or lump it, her body was in proportion. She salved her ego by deciding that if her boobs were any bigger, she'd probably just fall flat on her face every few minutes, anyway.

'Not that there's anyone to notice any of the above,' Flick reminded herself as she turned the hairdryer on. Ever since coming to America she'd kept well away from any romantic entanglements. It had been easy when she'd first arrived—she'd been engaged to Stuart, and so sure that he was the one. But as time wore on, it became pretty obvious that a whole bunch of things had pushed her and Stuart together, and none of them had been enough to base a marriage on. She'd been so messed up after what had happened with Steph and Marc Lambert, and she'd been estranged from her family …

Flick deliberately pushed the thought of her sister's ex-fiancé from her mind. Marc was the biggest mistake of her life, and reason enough to swear off men for a century or two.

Sliding her feet into her running shoes, Flick grabbed the backpack containing her work shoes, purse, and make-up bag. She always finished her hair and make-up at work so she looked her absolute freshest when she took charge of front of house operations at the hotel. As always, she felt a little thrill of satisfaction she had proven herself in this big, exciting city. Chloe Lambert had offered her an opportunity—a challenge, really. And she had taken it, and proved herself. Now she knew exactly what she wanted: her boss's job and then his boss's job. And so on, till she was managing a hotel or resort all on her own. She loved the hospitality industry, loved how portable it was and that she could get a job anywhere in the world. Still, she wasn't going anywhere for the next few years. There was still plenty to learn at Lassiter's Towers, and plenty of opportunity for advancement.

'Shelly, if you go out, make sure you use all the locks,' Flick said. Their father had visited a few months ago and insisted on installing two extra deadlocks; Flick was superstitiously certain that she would be burgled if she forgot to use them all.

Michelle rolled her eyes. 'As if they're going to stop someone if they really want to get in. They'll just climb the fire escape and smash the window.'

'Thank you, I know I'll sleep better with that image in mind,' Flick said dryly as she headed out the front door. 'Have a good day.'

Michelle's 'you too' echoed down the stairs after her. As usual, the various breakfast smells from the neighbours filled the stairwell: bacon and egg from Mr Mustaffa on level three, something with chilli and garlic from the Lees on level two, and something sweet and delicious from the ground floor. Flick paused to sniff the air appreciatively in the foyer. Apples? Spices? She couldn't quite work it out.

Giving up, she shouldered her way through the building's double doors and out into the street. Immediately she was swept up in the tide of people rushing along the busy streets of Manhattan. A big grin on her face, Flick slung her backpack onto her shoulders and matched her pace to the fast-walking New Yorkers around her. She'd fallen in love with this city. She loved the architecture, the rude people, the fashion, the pressure, the traffic—all of it. It was exciting, invigorating, scary and intimidating. 'About as different from Erinsborough as a girl could get,' she figured. But she was surviving here, holding her own. And now Shelly was living with her, and they could explore the million and one facets of the city together.

Michelle dusted the breadcrumbs off her sheets onto the floor then remembered the cockroaches. She'd only seen one since she moved in with Flick last week, and she never wanted to see another. Flick was vigilant with her anti-roach measures, leaving baits around and being very careful with food and garbage, but New York roaches were infamously hard to get rid of. With images of coffee-table-sized beasties having a party beneath her fold-out bed at night, Michelle grabbed the dustpan and broom and swept up the crumbs.

She then hauled herself into Flick's ridiculous bath and had a long shower. Her first class for the day didn't start till mid-morning, so there was no rush to get out the door. She was looking forward to graduating in six months' time. They got to wear robes and mortarboards with tassels, and she was definitely going to get Flick to take a photo of her throwing her cap in the air, just like in all those American teen movies.

Having carefully extracted herself out of the shower, Michelle dried herself off and examined her suitcase for clothing options for the day. It was still warm, even though it was autumn—no, fall—and she opted for jeans and a T-shirt. A wicked smile on her lips, she stole into Flick's room and filched her sister's denim jacket. What Flick didn't know wouldn't hurt her. Tucking her mobile phone into her back pocket and dropping money into her front, Michelle locked up the flat and started down the stairs. It was going to be so cool living here with Flick. Not that it hadn't been nice billeting with the Rolands in Jersey, but Jersey wasn't the city, no matter what anyone pretended, and every time she stayed the night with Flick, Michelle had realised that she was missing out. It had taken a few weeks of campaigning, but finally she'd convinced her sister to let her move in.

She was coming down the last flight of stairs when she smelt it. Something so amazing that her mouth started watering like crazy. Sniffing the air, Michelle followed the smell to the door of apartment number one.

'Wow,' she said under her breath, just as the door opened in her face and she found herself staring at a tall guy dressed in chef's checked pants and a black T-shirt. He was holding a white pastry box on his way out. Michelle felt herself flush, and hastily took a step back.

'Sorry. I just sort of followed the good smell …' she said lamely.

The guy looked pleased. 'Really? It smells good? Excellent!'

He had a typical American twang in his voice, and a shock of almost-red sandy hair. His eyes were brown, and when he smiled at her she noticed he had dimples.

'Hey, you just moved in upstairs, right?' he asked. He juggled the pastry box from his right hand to his left and extended his right hand in greeting. 'I'm Charlie.'

'Michelle,' she said, shaking his hand and wondering how he knew she'd just moved in.

'You're Australian!' Charlie suddenly said, as though he'd just worked out something really important and exciting.

Michelle was used to having her nationality pointed out to her at least two or three times a day. 'You're an Aussie!' people would say to her, pronouncing it 'Os-see'. Her personal favourite had been the time the woman stopped her on the bus and said, 'Gee, you speak good English.' Add to that the amount of times she'd been asked if she had a pet kangaroo, and the whole 'You're an Australian!' thing was getting a little old. So she was maybe a little sarcastic when she shot back at him:

'And you're an American!'

He looked offended. 'Canadian, thank you,' he corrected her.

'Same difference,' she said, eyes twinkling. She knew Canadians hated being mistaken for Americans.

'Right. So if I thought you were a New Zealander, you wouldn't mind?' he asked quickly.

This surprised a laugh out of Michelle. 'Someone knows his geography,' she said.

He put on a hick accent. 'They teach us good up there in the north.'

They smiled at each other, and Michelle tried to think of something else to say.

'So, were you baking?' she finally said.

'Oh yeah. I'm trying to come up with a new pastry dish for the restaurant where I work,' Charlie explained. 'I'm a sous chef, but my boss is a complete fascist and he won't let me experiment with the menu at all.'

He indicated the pastry box in his hand. 'This is part of my campaign to win him round.'

'Well, it smells pretty fantastic, whatever it is. Good luck,' Michelle said, turning away.

'You want to try one?' Charlie offered suddenly.

Michelle hesitated, severely tempted. 'I just brushed my teeth,' she said cautiously.

'So you don't want an apple and custard danish with a cinnamon glaze?' Charlie asked innocently, waving the box suggestively under Michelle's nose.

Michelle inhaled the scent of sugar and spice and felt her willpower dissolve.

'Maybe just a little taste.'

Charlie looked highly satisfied as he handed over a whole danish.

'Sorry, no knife,' he shrugged, conveniently forgetting he was standing in the doorway to his own apartment.

Michelle took a bite and closed her eyes. 'Yum.'

'Yeah? How yum? On a scale of one to ten, one being "just okay yum", ten being "I'd rather have this instead of sex yum"?'

Michelle's eyes popped open at the mention of sex.

'Um, it's really good,' she said, suddenly aware that she'd been standing there talking to Charlie for a while now. Feeling awkward, she handed the rest of her danish back to him.

'I've really got to go. Thanks for the taste test, though. And good luck,' she said.

For a second she thought she saw disappointment in his eyes, but then he smiled.

'Thanks for the feedback, Michelle,' he called after her as she pushed through the double doors and out into the street.

Michelle frowned to herself as she walked along. Her feet automatically turned her in the direction of the subway, and she cruised along on autopilot, trying to work out what had just happened back there with Charlie. One minute they'd been having a nice chat, then all of a sudden she just wanted to get out of there as quickly as possible.

She knew he'd only been joking with the sex thing. But still, it had made her feel uncomfortable which was stupid, because it wasn't as though he'd been trying to crack onto her or anything. Still, she admitted to herself that that was why she'd bailed on the conversation. Even though it had been a year since she'd left Connor and Erinsborough behind, she couldn't even contemplate the idea of dating. Flick, and her mum and all her friends at school assured her that she wouldn't love Connor forever, but she was beginning to have her doubts. He'd meant so much to her, and they'd been so close. Even now, just thinking of him brought a smile to her lips. But he'd insisted she come here and follow her dream. She was supposed to have gotten over him then fallen in love with some big hunky American football player or something stupid like that. But no one ever seemed to measure up to Connor O'Neil, and she was starting to suspect that they never would.

Flick smiled her widest smile as she approached the reception counter. She'd been called up from her office to deal with a guest complaint, and she had her charm ray set to 'stun'.

'Good afternoon, how can I help you?' she asked the portly middle-aged man who was standing waiting to one side, his brow puckered in annoyance.

'Are you the manager? I want to speak to the manager,' the man insisted.

Flick glanced down at the card on the desk that held the guest information.

'Mr Mendes, is that right? I'm the front of house manager. I deal with any guest queries or complaints as first port of call. If I'm unable to satisfy you, I'll certainly pass you on to my superior,' she explained smoothly. 'Jacobina on reception mentioned something to do with your mini-bar …?'

'Absolutely. It was a disgrace. It put me off my whole evening,' Mr Mendes said. He was flushed and a little damp around the brows, Flick saw, and she rapidly assessed him as a drama queen. No matter what, Mr Mendes was going to have his say and make a fuss and her job was to minimise the interruption to other guests.

Staying calm, she directed him to a set of comfortable seats to one side of the reception area. By the time she'd ordered Mr Mendes a complimentary latte, he'd finished explaining how he'd returned from his night out at the theatre feeling a little peckish, opened the pint of ice-cream in his mini-bar, and discovered that someone else had already been at it before him.

'Three big scoops missing! Absolutely blatant!' he said, jowls quivering with righteous indignation.

Flick had trouble keeping a straight face.

'That's truly terrible, and I'm sorry that you were put out like that, Mr Mendes. Being a big ice-cream fan myself, I totally understand your frustration. Now, how can I improve your stay with us? Apart from ensuring that tonight's ice-cream will, of course, be in pristine condition and on the house?'

She could see the colour settle in his face. It was like that a lot of the time with guests—most of them just wanting to be heard. She'd found over the years that asking them what they wanted as recompense was a far more effective way to calm them down than anything she could offer. Nine times out of ten they came back with very reasonable remedies or suggestions usually far less than what she was authorised to hand out.

'I don't need anything special. The point was more that someone has been trying to pull a fast one, and at my expense. If I hadn't felt like ice-cream, who's to say I wouldn't have been blamed by the next guest who discovered those missing scoops?' Mr Mendes said.

By the time Mr Mendes had drunk his coffee, Flick had him discussing his favourite ice-cream flavours, and had recommended her favourite gelati shop two blocks over.

'Best frozen yoghurt in town,' she assured him.

Mr Mendes tripped out the door a happy man, and Flick returned to the front desk.

'Thanks for that, Felicity,' Jacobina said.

'I'd have handled him myself, but I had a family of eight on my hands.'

'No worries. When you've got a moment, let housekeeping know that we'll have to get the maids to check the seals on the ice-creams from now on,' Flick said.

'Get out of town! I tell you, it amazes me how many different ways people can come up with to steal from hotels,' the receptionist said, shaking her perfectly coiffed hair.

Flick smiled her agreement and ran a practiced eye over the rest of the desk to make sure everything was running smoothly before heading back to her office. The remainder of the day was routine, and she left work with a spring in her step. Maybe she and Shelly could take in a movie tonight, or check out a show on Broadway. Sometimes stand-by tickets came up for the best things in town. Flick had seen some of the most dazzling shows on the cheap—Matthew Broderick in The Producers, Meryl Streep in an off-Broadway production.

Buzzing with plans, she took the stairs to the apartment two at a time.

'Honey, I'm home,' she called as she pushed open the front door.

She pulled up short when she realised the apartment was empty

'Oh.' She felt absurdly disappointed. It was one of the things she'd really looked forward to in having Michelle around: having someone at home when she got in from work.

'Grow up, you big girl's blouse,' she told herself as she shrugged off her backpack and toed off her sneakers. No doubt Michelle would be home soon enough and she'd be feeling claustrophobic about how small her apartment was with two people in it.

Grabbing a bottle of water from the fridge, Flick padded across to the sofa and reached for the remote control. As she passed the window, something out of the corner of her eye caught her attention. For a second her heart seemed to falter as she realised someone was on the fire escape outside the window. Michelle's offhand comment about someone breaking into the apartment raced across her mind, but then she recognised the huddled form as her sister.

'Shelly, what's wrong?' she said, ducking her head through the open double-hung window.

Straight away she realised Michelle had been crying and she quickly crawled out the window and sat next to her on the fire escape landing. 'What's happened? Are you all right?'

Michelle sniffed loudly and wiped at the tears on her cheeks. She looked very young and Flick felt a wave of affection for her youngest sister. Michelle might be opinionated and too big for her boots sometimes, but she was a sweet person and she really took things to heart.

'I got a letter from Connor today,' Michelle revealed, pushing the soggy pages towards Flick.

Flick stared down at Connor's messy handwriting. Up until he'd met her sister, Connor had been illiterate. Michelle had encouraged him to believe in himself and ask for help with his problem. Now this was how he repaid her, a four-page letter that made her cry.

'What did he say?' Flick asked angrily.

'He didn't say anything. His letter is great. It's beautiful. It's just full of … Connor, you know? I miss him so much, Flick.'

Michelle started crying again, and Flick slid an arm around her shoulder.

'Are you regretting your decision to leave him and come over here?' she asked carefully.

'No. Yes. Is it greedy to want to have everything?' Michelle asked, managing a weak smile through her tears.

Flick shrugged. 'More human than greedy, I think. The problem is, Shelly, that you did make your decision. You're here, and he's over there. There's not much you can do about it.'

'You don't think if I call him and tell him how I feel he might consider getting back together?' Michelle asked hopefully.

Flick squeezed her sister's shoulder and slowly shook her head.

'He's a young guy. Do you think it's fair to expect him to sit around waiting for you while you have the adventure of a lifetime over here? What would you do if the situation was reversed?'

'Tell him to get stuffed.'

'Exactly.'

Michelle nodded, and suddenly looked very determined. 'Okay, then I know what I have to do,' she said, pushing herself to her feet.

Flick felt the first faint tingling of alarm. 'What do you mean, Shelly?' she asked, following her sister through the window and back into the apartment.

Michelle was picking up the phone. 'I'm going home. I'm going to tell Connor I still love him, and if he still loves me I'm going to ask him to come back to New York with me.'

Flick kept her face carefully blank as she stepped forward and took the phone from her sister's hands.

'Just hold your horses for a minute, okay? You need to think this through a bit before you race off and buy a plane ticket. For starters, where are you going to get the money from? And what about your school?'

'I've still got some of Auntie Valda's money, and I'll only miss out on a few weeks of school. It'll be so cool, Flick. We can all live together. We can even get a bigger apartment. And Connor and I can go job hunting together.'

Michelle's eyes were shining with excitement now, and Flick felt a stab of concern for her. What if Connor didn't feel the same? Michelle was getting herself all worked up imagining a perfect future for her and Connor, and she had no idea how he felt. Or whether he was prepared to walk away from his new life in Australia to come to New York. Flick could see nothing but pitfalls ahead, but she didn't know what to say to stop Michelle from jumping in feet first. Feeling incredibly lame, she fell back on an old standard.

'Why don't you call Mum first and see what she thinks?' she suggested. 'She's the one who sees Connor all the time. And then maybe just think about it for a day or two before you make your final decision.'

She could see that Michelle didn't think much of the idea.

'I know exactly what Mum is going to say, and I don't want to hear it. I have to do this, Flick.'

Michelle's jaw was set, and Flick recognised her stubborn, determined look from many a childhood argument.

'At least call Mum and tell her that you're coming home,' Flick suggested, hoping that her mother would wheedle the truth out of Michelle.

No such luck. Although she could only hear one side of the conversation, it was clear that

Lyn was too excited about seeing her youngest daughter again to query the true purpose of the visit. When Michelle handed the phone over, she gave Flick a firm look that very clearly said 'not a word'. Flick rolled her eyes. If Michelle wanted to rush off on some impulsive trip back home, at the end of the day it was her business. Flick was hardly going to inform on her to their mother. Lyn had enough on her plate without having to deal with a squabble on the other side of the world.

'Hey, Mum,' she said into the phone.

It was nice to hear her mum's voice, and Flick talked to her for ten minutes before handing the phone back to Michelle. Although she didn't usually feel homesick, talking to Jack or her mum always left her feeling a little sad. She could hear baby Oscar playing in the background, and she reminded herself that she had to get home to have a cuddle with her new brother before he was too old to let her.

Finally, Michelle wound up the call and put the phone down with a decisive click.

'Now I just have to book my ticket,' she said.

Two days later, Flick watched Michelle walk through the doors into the passenger-only section of the airport. Almost as soon as her sister disappeared from view, a heavy feeling settled in her stomach. It was going to be strange without

Michelle around, even though they'd only been sharing for a few weeks. She'd become used to having her sister to spend time with, even if it was just hanging around watching TV. When she let herself back into the apartment and registered how down she was feeling, Flick tried to kick her melancholy mood. She'd been on her own for several months before Michelle came across with the exchange program. What had she done with herself then? Flick frowned as she remembered those first hard weeks. She'd been so determined to prove herself to Chloe Lambert that she'd worked like a dog, and because she'd been equally determined to make a go of things with Stuart, she'd rejected any and all offers to socialise from her work colleagues. As a result, she'd earned herself a reputation as a hard worker who kept to herself, and no one bothered to ask her out any more.

'Great. You're a social leper, Scully,' she told her empty apartment.

Because she wasn't a wallower, Flick put on her running shoes and three-quarter leggings, grabbed her iPod, and headed out for a run. Running was only a recent discovery, but Flick was fast becoming addicted. She loved the way she felt when she'd been pounding the pavement for half an hour—whether it was endorphins or just oxygen deprivation, it made her feel like she could fly. Today, she pushed herself and ran an extra block and a half than her normal route, and when she got back to the apartment she was drenched in sweat. Determined not to think about being alone, or the long evening that stretched ahead, she ran herself a bath and sank into it with a sigh. It might suck as a shower, but the bath absolutely came into its own when it was full of sudsy bubbles. Flick was drowsing in the steamy heat when the phone rang.

She was pathetically grateful to realise it was work, and that they wanted her to come in. As water pooled on the floorboards beneath her feet, Flick listened as the weekend manager explained that half the staff had gone down with food poisoning after attending Maria in housekeeping's engagement party last night. They were calling in all staff, including those in management. Flick assured a stressed out Sadie that she'd be in as soon as possible. She couldn't help smiling to herself, though—it seemed there were benefits to being a social leper after all, if it meant avoiding food poisoning.

There was an air of quiet desperation in the hotel when she arrived. She could sense it as soon as she entered, and she saw Jacobina's eyes widen with relief as she approached reception.

'Hallelujah, here comes the cavalry,' she said.

'You can't have her.' This was from Sadie as she swept in from the back office. 'I called her in, I need Felicity with me.'

'But we're short-handed on the desk!' Jacobina protested.

'You're down one person, and I'm down twenty! Do the math, girl,' Sadie argued.

Flick held up a hand. 'How about I help you both?' she suggested lightly, trying to defuse the situation.

Sadie just looked grumpy. 'I get her first,' she said, grabbing Flick by the elbow and leading her away.

'You ever worked in housekeeping?' she asked as she led Flick down into the staff-only part of the hotel.

'When I first started out, sure.'

They entered the female changing rooms, and Sadie eyed Flick up and down.

'You're about a size six, right?' she asked.

Flick did the translation into Australian sizing. 'Yeah, that's about right,' she agreed.

To her surprise, Sadie thrust a maid's uniform into her hands.

'Now I know you're front of house manager, Felicity, but I need housemaids. Is that going to be a problem for you?' she asked. Her expression told Flick that some of the other more senior staff members who'd been called in had objected to taking on such a menial task.

She smiled and took the uniform. 'Not a problem in the world.'

'I've got contract staff coming in to do most of the rooms, but I need someone with experience to tackle the penthouse suite and the prestige rooms. Two of them just need a freshen up, a dust and so on, because we're expecting guests this evening, but the penthouse will need a complete going over.'

'Cool, can do,' Flick nodded, already unbuckling her jeans and shrugging out of her T-shirt.

Sadie's shoulders sagged with relief. 'Felicity, I owe you big time. You ever need someone to come through for you, I am your girl,' she said.

Two minutes later, Flick was wearing the neat black and white uniform of a housemaid. It was a little short in the skirt she realised as she checked herself out in the mirror, but it was highly unlikely that she was going to bump into any guests working in the higher reaches of the hotel.

Tying on the old-school apron that completed the uniform, Flick quickly plaited her hair into a braid and fastened it down her back. Her running shoes were fine for this kind of work, so she left her dress shoes in her locker along with her street clothes.

'Here goes nothing,' she told her reflection. Three hours later, Flick backed out of the last of the prestige suites and swiped a hand across her forehead. She was a bit rusty on her housekeeping etiquette, she realised, and for a while she'd forgotten the right way to do everything. Then she remembered there was usually a checklist with the supply trolley, and she started doing everything by the book. It meant going back and doing a few things again, but she didn't want to let Sadie down which meant that now she was running late. Pushing her trolley into the lift, she stabbed urgently at the button for the penthouse. When the door just kept ringing at her, she suddenly remembered she needed to use her pass key to get the lift to go all the way to the top of the building. Rolling her eyes, she swiped her card and stabbed the button again. Everything for rich people had to be super-exclusive and perfect. Even though she knew better than most what sort of money changed hands for a night in the penthouse suite, Flick still thought it was pretty ridiculous to have the lift barred like this. There was a security door into the penthouse, the same as with the other rooms. Would it kill Mr and Mrs Important if one of the ordinary guests accidentally stepped out onto their floor, realised their mistake, and then got back in the lift? She didn't think so.

She was still marvelling at the demands of the rich and famous when she let herself into the penthouse. She simply stood there and gasped. It was an awe-inspiring suite, that was for sure—lavish décor, floor-to-ceiling windows, the best of everything. But that wasn't what took her breath away. Littered across every conceivable surface in the main living area were glasses, plates of food, platters, ashtrays, and a host of other party paraphernalia. Someone had thrown a big party in the penthouse, and left it for someone else to clean up. And today that lucky person was Flick.

Her mouth open, Flick did a quick tour of the whole suite. The kitchen was a disaster, and two of the three bedrooms had also seen some heavy-duty partying. Flick returned to her trolley with a grim set to her mouth. This was going to take some serious elbow grease.

Two hours later, she'd vacuumed, dusted, wiped, cleared and fluffed her way through everything except the master bathroom. Her hair had come loose from its braid, and she'd long since discarded the stupid apron. Now she surveyed the carnage in the bathroom through narrowed eyes. She started by making a pile of all the dirty towels. She didn't want to imagine how many people must have enjoyed the shell-shaped spa bath in order to use all those towels. Instead, she sprayed a vat-load of disinfectant on the spa and hosed it off using the hand-shower fitting. This proved to be so effective that she decided to use the same technique in the enormous double shower when she realised it was also fitted with a hand-shower. Her plan came slightly unstuck, however, when she discovered the intimidating looking tap fittings that graced the shower wall. There were at least eight water jets, and a whole bank of mixers and buttons to choose from. Picking up the hand-shower from its bracket, she tried the first control and received a face full of cold water for her troubles. She jumped backwards, almost slipping on the wet floor. Spluttering, she recovered and studied the complicated array of buttons, taps and jets. Convinced she'd worked it out, she pressed another button, and this time all six jets sprayed water at her while the hand-shower remained frustratingly dry.

'Stupid bloody thing!' she cursed, stabbing at the button to stop the flow of cold water.

Her uniform was dripping wet, and she realised that water had leaked out all over the main floor of the bathroom. Swearing under her breath, Flick exited the shower, sneakers squelching, and grabbed the hand-shower from the spa bath. Unfortunately, the hose didn't quite make it all the way to the shower enclosure. Flick cursed under her breath again. Pulling the flexible hose as far as she could, she aimed it inside the shower cubicle and turned the water on full blast. As she'd hoped, it still proved effective, and after a few minutes the shower cleaner was washed away. She turned the water off with a cocky, self-satisfied flick of her hand.

'Take that, smarty pants,' she said, blowing on the end of the hand-shower like a gunslinger blowing smoke away from his freshly fired pistol.

The sound of slow, lazy applause surprised her and she spun on her heel to find herself facing a six-foot-two tall, handsome male. Dark-haired and blue-eyed, he was slouched in the doorway, and had clearly been there for quite some time.

'Interesting, if a little unorthodox,' he said, white teeth flashing in a smile.

'And just who the hell are you?' Flick demanded.

Chapter 2

*H*arrison Lambert couldn't help himself. He grinned, his gaze running up and down the soaking wet woman standing in front of him. She was beautiful, he decided. The uniform clung to her in all the right places, and her clear brown eyes flashed defensively at him. Her legs were long and slim, and he liked the way she carried herself—head high, chin out a bit. Like she was ready to take on anyone.

'Harrison Grant,' he lied smoothly, dangling the room key he'd just picked up from reception. 'This is my room for the night.'

Her mouth formed a silent 'o' of surprise, and he watched in fascination as colour stole into her cheeks. Stunning, not merely beautiful, he corrected himself.

'I'm so sorry!' she said. 'I didn't realise it was so late. We're short-handed today …' She smiled weakly. 'If you could just give me another ten minutes, I'll be finished in here.'

'Sure, but don't rush on my account,' he shrugged, resisting the urge to run his eyes up those long, brown legs again.

Pushing himself away from the doorframe, he nodded his goodbye and headed back to the master bedroom. She was Australian, he realised. It was good to hear an Australian voice after so long in the States. He wondered how she'd gotten a job in the hotel; it was unlikely that they would sponsor her for a work permit for such a menial job. She must have a Green Card, or maybe she was married to an American. He didn't like this last thought, and he was frowning as he tugged open the zipper on his suit bag.

He hung his suits up automatically, unable to keep his mind off the maid. He estimated she was in her early twenties, but there was a wariness in her eyes that told him she'd seen a few things. Not jaded, or world-weary but definitely cautious. He realised he was smiling again; he liked a challenge.

The sound of the housekeeping cart trundling down the hall towards the door brought him out of the bedroom. She was doing a

last check of the lounge area, straightening some
magazines and adjusting the position of a vase full
of fresh flowers. Her blonde hair was hanging in
wet tendrils down her back, and a few choice
strands were stuck to her cheek and neck.

'All done?' he asked, and she started and
pressed a hand to her heart.

'Sorry,' he apologised, realising he'd taken
her by surprise. 'This carpet's about three feet
thick. No sound.'

'Nothing but the best in the penthouse,' she
said lightly.

'Does that go for the maids as well?' he
heard himself ask, almost wincing at his own line.
'Nice one, Harrison. Really smooth and original,'
he thought.

She didn't know what to do with his
comment, he noticed. Her eyes studied him
warily.

'We try our best,' she finally said, moving
back towards the housekeeping cart.

He didn't want her to go.

'Hang on a minute,' he said, reaching into
his pocket for his wallet. Fumbling, he pulled out
a ten-dollar note and walked towards her. 'Here.
For a job well done.'

Her eyes widened, and she stared at the
money in his hand like it was poisoned.

'No,' she said abruptly.

'No?'

'Definitely no,' she repeated. 'I don't need a tip for doing my job.'

'That's very Australian of you. Hasn't anyone ever told you that you live off your tips in America?' he asked.

'But I don't deserve a tip,' she said. 'I'm running late, and I made a mess in the bathroom. You'd be wasting your money.'

'Maybe I see things differently. Maybe I'm glad you were running late,' he said.

Her head cocked to one side then, and a light came into her eyes as she realised he was flirting with her.

'Are you always this forthright?' she challenged him.

'Yes. When I want something.'

The light danced in her eyes now. She was enjoying this as much as he was.

'Sometimes people don't always get what they want. Ask the Rolling Stones, they wrote a whole song about it.'

'Clearly they didn't have the staying power.'

'And you do?' she asked, one hand on her hip.

'Absolutely. Never give up, never surrender,' he said.

A smile tugged at the corners of her mouth.

'Sounds like a line from *Braveheart*. He died in the end, too, didn't he?'

'Another man with no stamina.'

She laughed, and the sound seemed to surprise her. Suddenly she seemed more aware of her surroundings, and the light died in her eyes. Her body tensed, and she nodded her head slightly.

'I really have to get going,' she said.

He couldn't think of anything else to say, and abruptly he was aware of how bad this must look—the high-flying penthouse guest trying to horn onto the maid. 'Would it be any better if she knew the truth?' he asked himself. Because he knew what the answer was and didn't like it, he simply watched her go.

It wasn't until the door clicked shut behind her that he realised he was still holding onto his ten dollars.

Flick pressed her back against the closed door of the penthouse and took a deep breath. Her heart was pounding in her chest, and she felt like she'd just run a mile.

'What was I thinking?' she asked herself. For just a few moments there, she had forgotten who she was, and where she was. She'd allowed herself to get caught up in the teasing, knowing glint in a handsome stranger's eyes.

She'd actually blinked a few times when she first saw him standing there in the bathroom. He was very attractive, with his clear blue eyes, dark lashes, and dark, wavy hair. He wore his suit well, the navy pinstriped fabric draping perfectly off his broad shoulders. There was something about the look in his eyes, a certain challenging light, a knowingness that had caught her attention and held it.

She'd been unable to stop thinking about him the whole time she tidied the rest of the master bathroom. Then, just as she was about to wheel the trolley back out the door, she'd caught sight of her reflection in the bathroom mirror. She'd stifled a groan. While she'd been standing there doing mental hubba-hubbas over him, he'd been checking out the drowned rat that stared back at her from the mirror. Her uniform was stuck to her in ungainly wrinkles, and her hair was a disaster. So much for the glint she'd thought she'd seen in his eye.

Then he'd approached her out in the living room. And she'd flirted with him. And not just harmless flirting, world championship flirting. Full-on Bogey and Bacall flirting.

Flick closed her eyes, mortified at her own behaviour. She didn't even know the man from Adam, and she'd been bantering with him like some desperado. Ugh.

Flick levered herself away from the door and pushed the trolley towards the lift with more verve than necessary. It slammed into the wall, and Flick grimaced, quickly checking the wall to make sure there was no damage. Fortunately, she'd clipped the metal framing on the lift doors, and she relaxed a little.

All the way down in the lift she kept having flashes of her conversation with Harrison Grant. Her toes curled in her sneakers as she remembered the way she'd had her hand on her hip as she sassed back at him.

'Very classy, Felicity,' she chastised herself. 'Really top shelf.'

Thank God he was only staying one night. He'd probably check out in the morning, and unless she was very unlucky, she need never see the handsome and ridiculously charming Mr Grant again. Her stomach dipped a little with disappointment, but she squashed the feeling ruthlessly. She was glad he was going tomorrow; it saved making a fool of herself again.

'Whoa—what happened to you?' Sadie asked as she returned the trolley to the housekeeping department.

'Little problem with the penthouse suite,' Flick said dryly.

Sadie frowned. 'I thought you were finished in there ages ago. Hell, we sent the guest up half an hour ago!'

'Yeah, I know, I met him,' Flick said, lifting her damp hair off the back of her neck.

Sadie's eyes rounded. 'Woops. Did it all work out okay?'

Flick deliberately didn't think about those few moments of hard-core flirtation.

'It was fine. The previous guests were pigs, though. Looks like they had a party up there last night.'

'You should have called down for reinforcements,' Sadie said guiltily. 'You shouldn't have had to do it all yourself.'

'Did you suddenly get an extra crew of staff in?' Flick asked, reminding the woman of why she'd been playing housemaid in the first place.

Sadie shrugged a shoulder, acknowledging Flick's point.

'You go now, though. You've done more than your fair share. The other managers disappeared hours ago.'

Flick smiled her thanks and didn't bother telling Sadie that she'd been more than happy to do the work—anything was better than spending the day wondering why her life felt so empty all of a sudden.

Flick popped her head in upstairs to ensure the front desk was coping with being a staff member down, but Jacobina was all smiles so she headed down again to change into her street clothes. She was so clammy from the wet uniform that she had a shower then gave her hair a quick once-over with the blow-dryer so she wouldn't catch cold on the way home. The days were still warm enough at the moment, but at night the cold could really creep up on you.

Five minutes later she was dressed in faded denim jeans and a pink T-shirt, with her black oriental silk embroidered bomber jacket over the top. Her hair was long and loose down her back, and she slung her backpack over her shoulder, ready to go.

Waving goodbye to Jacobina on the desk, she stepped out into the gathering twilight. Yellow cabs rushed past, their headlights a blur, and the buildings around her twinkled with a hundred lights as darkness crept in. She was about to turn in the direction of the apartment when something made her hesitate. If she went home right now, she'd just sit in front of the television and channel surf. Even though she felt pleasantly tired after all the cleaning, she didn't feel like she could face a night on the sofa. Maybe she should go down to Times Square, see what was going on. Maybe there would be a movie she could see.

A few years ago, she'd thought there was nothing sadder in the world than going to a movie on her own. Back then, Flick had had trouble getting by without having a boyfriend in her life.

Times had changed, and now she went to the movies on her own pretty regularly.

Decision made, she swung on her heel and started walking in the opposite direction, long blonde hair swinging behind her.

Harrison exited the hotel and took a deep breath of dirty, polluted, exciting New York air. He'd been on the west coast for too long. He was really looking forward to spending the next six months in Manhattan. Refurbishing the Lassiter's Towers to take it from five stars up to six stars was a big job, but something he was more than qualified to handle. He was thirty years old now, and had been working in the family business since he graduated from university at twenty-one. He'd done a stint in most roles in the hotel industry, and for the past five years had helped manage the fifteen Lassiter's hotels that dotted the USA.

Normally he'd have hand-balled this job onto one of his senior project managers, but it suited him to be out of LA just now. His lips thinned as he thought of his soon-to-be-ex-wife Amanda. She would take advantage of his absence to start showing-off her new man about town. A change for her, after all the months of skulking around in hotels. No doubt Amanda had thought she was being loyal by using her husband's family's hotel chain to accommodate her sordid little affair.

He'd seen it differently when he'd caught his wife of five years kissing her lover in the forecourt of the Lassiter's Grand Plaza in Beverley Hills.

Even though it was five months ago, the memory still filled him with rage. He'd given her his heart, and she'd handed it back to him with a sneer. Thank God they hadn't had children. That was the only blessing he could find in the whole mess. Of course, that wouldn't stop her from going for as much of the family money as she could get her talons on in the divorce, but she'd have a rude awakening on that front. His parents were canny business people, and all of the family funds were tied up in trusts. Amanda was going to be very disappointed if she thought she was going to spit him out and walk away the richer for it.

Harrison realised that he'd automatically started walking towards Times Square. He'd planned on catching a cab across town to spend the evening in one of his clubs, but a walk was probably a good idea. It had been a long flight, and it would be good to clear his head.

He'd been walking for half a block when he saw her. At first he wasn't sure— her hair was loose and she was in jeans and a black jacket, and not a sopping wet maid's uniform. But then she stopped to look in a shop window and he saw her profile. It was definitely her.

She looked great in jeans. They sat low on her hips and snugly hugged her bottom. She was wearing some silky bomber-jacket thing, and her blonde hair was spread out across it like jewellery displayed for sale. Very attractive. Flirting with her had been a matter of sheer instinct when he'd first seen her up in the hotel room—she was there, she was beautiful, he'd been attracted. But now he assessed the situation more pragmatically. She was an employee of the hotel. By extension, his employee: a lowly one, but an employee just the same. In all his years in the business, he'd never mixed business with pleasure. His thoughts briefly ran to his younger brother, Marc. Marc had strayed with an employee once—and it had cost him his marriage.

Ahead of him, she turned away from the window and started walking again. He watched the sway of her hips and backside as she walked, almost hypnotised by the motion. He remembered the flirtatious light in her eyes, and began to make excuses for himself. For starters, at this point in time she had no idea that his family owned the hotel she worked in. That was the whole point of checking in under a false name; as Harrison Grant he was far better able to assess the performance of staff and the hotel in general than if he walked in the door as Harrison Lambert. The pretence would be over tomorrow when he announced himself to the hotel manager, but tonight they were free and clear. And tomorrow? Well, as a very senior manager in the hotel chain, he didn't rub shoulders with housemaids on a regular basis. There was probably very little chance that their paths would ever cross again, if he chose to make it that way. And he was only here for six months, after all.

Before his decision was consciously made he started striding, long legs eating up the ground to catch up to her. He waited until she stopped in front of another window before making his move. Casually moving to stand beside her, he eyed the long tan trench coat on the Donna Karan model assessingly.

'You'd look better in black, if you ask me,' he said, and she turned to him with startled eyes.

It was him. Harrison what's-his-name from the penthouse suite. Flick stared up at him for a moment, completely lost for words. He just smiled down at her.

'And it won't keep you warm enough, either,' he said, indicating the trench coat she'd been lusting after. 'Too thin. You'll need something really thick to survive your first New York winter.'

Somehow she found her voice. 'This will be my second winter,' she said.

'Yeah? Somehow you look like you just got here—kind of fresh,' he said.

Flick frowned, suddenly wary. Did he think she was a pushover or something? Then she remembered the way she'd carried on in the penthouse. Of course he thought she was a pushover! She'd practically done a striptease for him back there.

'Listen,' she said, deciding to end this here and now. 'Before, up in the penthouse … That was a mistake, okay? It's not going to happen again.'

She held his eyes so he'd know she was serious.

'Good,' he said, surprising her. 'I'm not particularly proud of myself for coming across as the world's biggest sleazoid. Let's just pretend it never happened and start all over again.'

He smiled at her, and Flick realised he was holding out his hand, wanting to seal their discussion with a handshake.

'Harrison Grant, pleased to meet you,' he said.

She slid her hand into his automatically, not really thinking. His skin felt warm and firm as it closed around hers.

'I'm Flick,' she managed before an electric thrill raced up her arm and she jerked her hand back. If he noticed her reaction, he didn't say anything.

'So, Flick, have you eaten?' he asked.

'No.' The word was out before Flick could stop herself. 'Before you wanted to stop yourself, liar,' she thought.

'Me either. You want to go somewhere?'

He was being really careful not to come across as a sleaze, she could tell. And he wasn't. He was coming across as a really, really attractive guy who was smiling down at her asking her out. And she was feeling a bit weak in the knees and definitely weak in the willpower department.

'Like where?' she hedged, shifting from one foot to the other awkwardly.

'Pizza? Pasta? Filet Mignon? Your call. I'm your culinary slave for the evening,' he offered.

Now he was being funny. Flick shot another look up at his face, and got caught in his intense blue gaze.

'Okay,' she said.

He sagged comically. 'Had me worried there for a moment, Flick. I hate eating alone.'

'Me, too,' she said. It was true, even though she'd done a lot of it the past year or so.

'So, which is it? Which way are we going?' he asked, spreading his hands wide to indicate it was all up to her.

She tried to think, but her stomach was so busy hosting a butterfly square-dance that she came up blank.

'I don't know, you choose,' she said.

He pursed his lips for a moment, considering. Her eyes were drawn to his mouth, and she saw that he had firm, full lips, the bottom one slightly fuller than the top. Nice.

'Okay. I'm thinking greasy burger, crispy

chips, big thick shakes that give you ice-cream headaches. How does that sound?'

Flick's stomach made a rude noise, and she felt herself blush.

'Um, good?' she interpreted for her belly.

To her relief, he laughed. 'It's up this way a little,' he said, indicating with his head.

They started walking, him matching his longer stride to hers. After a few steps she felt a tug on her backpack.

'Here, let me take that for you,' he said.

Flick suddenly found herself smiling hugely at his display of old-fashioned courtesy.

'What's so funny?' he asked, smiling back.

He had a great smile, too. Strong white teeth, and a cheeky light in his eyes that said he was really enjoying himself.

'Nothing. It's just that was really gallant of you,' Flick teased him.

'Gallant? You think I was being gallant?'

'Or maybe you were being chivalrous, and the next thing I know, you'll be throwing your jacket down over a puddle so I won't get my shoes muddy.'

'Not this jacket. No way. I might direct you around the puddle though. Would that still count as chivalry?'

'It's not quite the same, is it? A little traffic direction versus a serious fashion sacrifice,' she said.

'Too true. I think you're on the money there,' he agreed.

He flashed her a look out of the corner of his eyes, and she laughed again.

'So after all that, does that mean I get to carry your bag for you?' he asked after a few moments of silence.

Flick shook her head. 'I can carry my own bag, thanks,' she said firmly.

'Ah,' he said, looking very knowing.

Flick sensed some payback teasing in the offing, but she couldn't resist the bait.

'Ah what?'

'You're a "I can carry my own bag" kind of girl. I should have known,' he said. 'I bet you're going to argue over who's going to pay the bill, too.'

Flick tried to look as though this was the furthest thing from her mind, even though she'd just done a mental cash check to ensure she had enough to cover her share of the tab.

'I might surprise you. I might order the most expensive burger on the menu, and the biggest shake they've got, and stick you with the bill and send you bankrupt at the end of the evening.'

'Go on, I dare you,' he said, and suddenly she remembered that he was staying in the penthouse suite and that going bankrupt over a few burgers was probably not a big concern of his.

It made her suddenly wonder if she was doing the right thing, having a meal with him like this. Although it wasn't an official policy of the hotel, it was generally accepted that staff would not socialise with guests. Especially not the really high-powered, high-flying ones who occupied the suites on the top floor of the hotel. The last thing the hotel wanted was their big clients staying away over some awkwardness with staff.

'So, Flick, what brings you to New York?' he asked after the silence had stretched between them for a few moments.

'I got a job offer, and it didn't seem like something I could walk away from,' she said.

He frowned, and she got the feeling he was going to ask her something but she beat him to it.

'What brings you to New York?' she asked.

'Business, what else?' he said. 'But I'm hoping to get a bit of R and R in, too.'

'Have you ever noticed how nobody who lives in New York actually seems to have been born here?' Flick mused as they turned the corner and entered a cross street. 'Not one single person who works at the hotel is a native New Yorker.'

He considered it for a moment.

'It's like that with a lot of big cities though.

People arrive, try their luck, then they move on. Maybe they go home again when they feel like they've proven something to themselves.'

Flick nodded. In the back of her mind, she always imagined going back to Australia at some stage.

'You look like you agree with me,' he fished.

'Sure. Australia's always going to be home,' she said.

'Yeah, me too,' he agreed.

She shot him a startled look. 'But you're not Australian!' she said.

'Bloody oath I am, mate,' he said in a broad Aussie drawl.

Flick gaped at him. 'But you don't sound like an Australian,' she said, mystified that she hadn't recognised a fellow ex-patriot.

'Years of overseas schooling. Half here, half in the UK. So now I've got this very acceptable mid-Atlantic accent going on.'

'Hmmpph,' Flick said, feeling vaguely put out that she hadn't guessed for herself.

'Here we are,' he said, and she saw they were standing in front of a typical greasy-spoon type New York diner.

The place was pretty crowded, but they scored a booth up the back and quickly ordered their food. Flick was starving and excited all at once, and she suspected she wasn't going to be able to do justice to her order. The man sitting opposite her had her stomach tied in knots. The fact that he was actually a fellow Aussie only added to her feelings of attraction. And then there was the fact that he was a successful man. Before, she'd only ever really dated boys—except for Stuart and Marc, of course. But Stuart had been a country boy, worlds away from the suit-garbed man sitting across from her. If anything, Marc was the closest she'd come to the sort of man Harrison appeared to be—but Marc seemed unsure and untried when she compared him with Harrison. There was an edge to Harrison, a sort of restless energy and authority that Marc would never possess.

Flick realised that her thoughts had strayed to Marc Lambert again, and she wondered why he'd been popping up into her thoughts so much lately. For a long time now she hadn't given him a second thought, and now she was out with a new, interesting man and she was thinking about how she'd almost ruined her sister's life.

Maybe it was a bad sign. Maybe on some instinctive level she understood that this man was bad for her. Eyeing the door, Flick wondered how embarrassing it would be if she made her excuses and hightailed it out of there.

Harrison realised that something was wrong. It surprised him that he could read her so easily on such a short acquaintance, but he could. She was thinking about something sad. The light had gone out of her eyes, and she was sitting stiffly, her eyes darting to the door. He didn't know how he knew, but he guessed she was thinking of bailing on him. And he realised that he didn't want that to happen. She was a fascinating woman—beautiful, spirited, funny. Clever, too, although something told him she would be surprised to hear him say that.

'Here's what I'm thinking,' he said when he saw Flick reach for her backpack, confirming his guess that she was about to leave. 'You wait until you get your burger, you check it out to see if it's worth all the fuss, and then you decide if you still want to go or not.'

She stared at him. 'How did you know?'

'Apart from the fact that you look like a bunny in the car headlights? I don't know,' he said lightly.

She relaxed a little at his light tone. 'I just realised that this is probably a really bad idea.'

Even though part of him agreed with her, he couldn't let that rest.

'Why?' he challenged.

'Well, the hotel wouldn't like it, for starters. And I'm not very good at this sort of thing,' she said vaguely.

'Well, I'm no star in the romance stakes, either, so we're matched there,' he said, unable to keep the edge of bitterness out of his voice.

She gave him a look, but didn't ask. He was grateful, and he realised it meant he couldn't go hunting for her ghosts, either. That suited him just fine.

'We're just having a burger, Flick. A bit of minced beef, some high cholesterol cheese that for some reason the Americans insist on dying bright orange, and some pickle that we'll probably both leave on the plate. It's no big deal.'

'I like the pickle,' she said, and he realised she was going to stay.

She had amazing eyes he noticed, now that he could sit opposite her and really enjoy them. Like french-polished mahogany, clear and glowing. And she had lovely bone structure, with broad, sweeping cheekbones. Beautiful.

Thankfully their meals came before he made a fool of himself or sent her bolting for the door. After much negotiation she traded some of her fries for his unwanted pickle, and then tucked into her meal. He watched with approval as she demolished her burger, completely unconcerned about the fact that she had sauce smeared on her chin as she argued with him over the latest Hugh Grant movie.

By the time they were standing on the sidewalk again, he was absolutely positive that he didn't want to let her go just yet. More then anything he'd like to take her back to his hotel room and make love to her—he couldn't remember being this attracted to a woman in a long time. Not that he'd been looking while he was married, but the point remained, nonetheless. She was very desirable and he was absolutely certain that if he suggested they go back to his room she would turn him down flat.

Because he knew that would also be the end of their time together, he suggested instead that they continue on down to Times Square. She readily agreed, and they dawdled their way down the street, laughing at each other's jokes, teasing, getting to know each other.

Once in the Square he talked her into a movie, choosing a horror flick with ruthless calculation. But, instead of cowering against him and giving him an excuse to put his arm around her shoulders, she kept grabbing his knee unexpectedly during the tense scenes, deliberately startling the hell out of him. As they left the cinema she explained with a grin that she had a couple of good friends who were into horror movies when she was younger. He suspected that the Tad and Paul she talked about had probably watched them with her for exactly the same reason that he had.

Still loathe to let her go, he bought her a coffee and a slice of sticky date cake in another diner, and she insisted that he eat half of it. Because they only had one fork, she wound up feeding him the cake. It was hardly a seduction scene, though—she kept 'accidentally' smearing the cake on his cheeks or lips as she was conveying it to his mouth. Of course, he had to retaliate, grabbing the fork from her hand and smearing a trail of sticky syrup across her cheek.

As they exited the diner and both automatically turned in the direction of the hotel, Harrison realised that he was completely and utterly charmed. Flick was a fascinating mixture of womanly intrigue and tomboyish mischief. And he desperately wanted to spend the night with her.

It took Flick a moment to realise they were standing out the front of the Lassiter's Towers. She'd been so rapt up in talking to Harrison that she'd lost track of where they were. Now she skittered a look up at him and quickly looked away again.

'Well, this is you,' she said, nervously fiddling with her wristwatch. 'I'm further up that way.'

She waved a hand vaguely towards the other end of the street.

She'd had a great night. He was the funniest, most interesting and charming man she'd met in a long time. She found him powerfully attractive. And she was deeply afraid of what she'd be tempted to do if he kissed her.

That thought in mind, she took a step backwards, determined to avoid temptation.

'I had a great time,' she said. 'It was really nice meeting you.'

She sounded like an idiot, she knew. He just smiled at her, and reached for the straps of her backpack where they looped over each shoulder. Before she could say anything, he used the straps to haul her close.

And then he was kissing her. Flick closed her eyes, and gave herself up to the most intense, passionate, promising kiss of her life. Harrison's hands slid from her shoulders up into her hair, and he angled her head back and tantalised her with his mouth.

When he finally pulled away she was out of breath and it took her a moment to make her eyes open. He was still standing close, and he peppered her face with light kisses, one hand still tangled in her hair. Instinctively she let her head tilt to one side as he found the tender skin at the base of her ear.

'Come upstairs with me, Flick,' he breathed into her neck.

Parts of Flick screamed a big fat yes, but she managed to bite back on the words. Reluctant, she placed the palm of her hand flat on his chest. His body felt warm and strong through the fine silk of his shirt, and for a second she hesitated before finally pushing him away.

'I'm sorry, I can't,' she said simply.

For a moment she sensed he wanted to argue with her, to try and convince her, but then he just nodded his head in agreement. Ducking his head, he pressed one last, searing kiss to her lips before stepping away.

'Good night, Flick,' he said.

She stared at him for a moment, so tempted—too tempted—to change her mind. Then she forced herself to turn away and start walking.

She could feel him watching her, and she pressed a hand to her lips, remembering his kiss. Was she making a mistake, walking away from him like this?

But Flick couldn't do it any other way. She wasn't someone who just jumped into bed as though it didn't mean anything. If Harrison liked her, he'd find a way to see her again.

She smiled into the darkness as she walked. She had a feeling that tonight was the start of something really special.

Chapter 3

*H*arrison woke up early and went for a run along the still-dark streets of Manhattan. He put his bad night's sleep firmly at the door of the bewitching and elusive Flick. Still, he was in town for six months. He could take her out again, kiss those pouty lips of hers a few more times. He had the feeling that she could be pretty passionate under the right circumstances. He just had to find them.

As he was stepping out of the shower a little later, it occurred to him that perhaps it wasn't just straight-out, unadulterated carnal desire that he was feeling. After all, if that was the case, why was he wondering whether she'd enjoy a night out at the Starlight Room? And why was he imagining skating with her on Rockefeller Plaza once winter set in? She'd look incredibly cute in mittens and a fuzzy hat, he guessed.

Knotting his tie and checking his reflection in the mirror, Harrison reminded himself that he was in the middle of a messy divorce. The last thing he wanted was to start up something with a hotel employee. Wasn't it?

Feeling thoroughly unsettled, Harrison took the lift down to the foyer. He had an appointment with the hotel manager for breakfast, and he crossed the marble-floored, echoing foyer to the in-house restaurant. He was about to step into the carpeted restaurant entrance when a flash of blonde caught the corner of his eye. Instinctively he turned, hoping it was Flick despite all his good intentions. But the figure walking briskly towards the reception desk was dressed in the hotel's corporate uniform, and her hair was neatly pinned up on the back of her head. Not Flick, obviously. Then she turned her head slightly, and he saw the familiar slope of a cheekbone. He frowned, staring after the tall, slim woman. Surely there couldn't be two women with such striking bone structure working in the same hotel?

'Harrison, great to see you.'

Harrison swivelled around to find the hotel's manager, Leo Burns, waiting for him in the entrance to the hotel restaurant. He'd worked with Leo before, and considered him a friend as well as a colleague.

'I've got a table set up for us, come on through,' Leo said.

'Great. Thanks,' Harrison said absently.

He threw another glance over his shoulder, but the woman was long gone. He realised Leo was leading the way to a table near the window, and he followed, his mind whirring at a million miles an hour.

'Now, how do you want to handle this? You want to eat, and I'll fill you in on our projected bookings for the next six months? Or did you have something else in mind?' Leo asked as they sat down.

'Bookings are a good place to start. But I do have one question for you. There was a blonde girl walking past just now. Early twenties, one of your managers.'

Leo looked bemused. 'Blonde? Sadie in charge of housekeeping's blonde, but she's a little older.'

'Is she Australian?' Harrison asked quickly.

Leo's face cleared. 'You mean Felicity! She's front of house manager. A real dynamo.'

Harrison felt something hard settle in his stomach. 'Felicity? Not Felicity Scully?' he asked flatly.

It made sense, of course. Flick, short for Felicity. He would have worked it out for himself if he'd been using his brains instead of thinking with another part of his anatomy. He knew she'd been given a role in one of the New York properties. What she'd been doing cleaning his room when she was a manager he had no idea, but it was irrelevant.

The important thing was that she was the deceitful, faithless woman who'd destroyed his brother's wedding. He'd been caught up in family business at the time, but he could clearly remember his mother's description of the whole sordid affair. Felicity had gone behind her own sister's back and his brother Marc had been so bent out of shape with her game playing that he'd walked away from his bride at the altar. It had been a disaster, pure and simple—and all because Felicity Scully had been unable to keep her hands off her sister's fiancé. Worse still, when Marc had tried to take her up on what had been offered before the wedding, Felicity had blown him off for yet another man.

He felt his face harden as he remembered the apparent innocence of her behaviour last night. Suddenly her charming modesty was shown for what it was: just a ploy to get a man hooked so she could lead him around by the nose.

'Harrison …?'

He snapped back to reality, and realised that Leo had been asking him something.

'Sorry,' he said stiffly.

'You want a cooked breakfast, or are you happy with the buffet?' Leo asked.

Harrison shook his head dismissively. Suddenly he'd lost his appetite.

'I'll just have coffee for now.'

Leo was looking at him intently, sensing something was up.

'You don't know her, do you? I know your mother was instrumental in getting her over here initially. Felicity has more than proven herself since then, hence her promotion to managing front of house.'

Harrison forced a casualness he didn't feel. 'It's nothing. She just reminded me of someone, that's all,' he said.

Leo seemed to accept this, launching into a detailed explanation of the hotel's booking commitments for the next six months. Harrison would have to juggle the renovation work around the accommodation requirements, and he forced himself to pay attention to Leo's words.

Felicity Scully would keep.

Flick hummed a little tune to herself as she checked over the reports from the weekend. Apart from the wave of food poisoning that had taken out half the staff, the front of house operations had run as smoothly as clockwork. Running her eye down the accommodation bookings for the next few days, Flick concentrated on finding hot spots that would require additional staff. Tour groups booking in, large groups checking out, any unusual load on the reception or concierge staff; it was her job to predict high demand periods and plan around them.

'You sound pretty pleased with yourself.'

It was Jacobina, buttoning on her neat uniform jacket in the office doorway. Flick lifted a shoulder casually. 'Just happy, that's all.'

Jacobina raised a well-plucked eyebrow at her. 'Crapola.' Entering Flick's office properly, she parked a hip against the desk and crossed her arms. 'Come on, give. You met someone, didn't you?'

Flick couldn't quite hold Jacobina's eye, or stop the little smile that curved her mouth.

'I knew it! You've just got that look. Kind of smug. In a nice way,' Jacobina said.

'Don't get too carried away. I'm probably never going to see him again,' Flick said ruefully.

'Sweetheart, have you had a look at yourself lately? No man is going to walk away from something as fine as you, trust me.'

Flick rolled her eyes. Jacobina was always encouraging her to get out and socialise more. She seemed to think it was her personal responsibility to find Flick a boyfriend.

'Thanks, J.B., but I think I had my chance and I blew it.'

'Let me guess—he wanted 'coffee', and you said no.'

Flick stared at her. 'How do you know this stuff?'

'Girlfriend, I read a lot, and I watch a lot of daytime TV. Don't you worry your pretty little head about saying no to Mr Hot-and-Heavy. If you never see him again because you said no, you know you did the right thing.'

In her heart, Flick knew that Jacobina was right. But she couldn't stop thinking about him.

'He'll call,' Jacobina suddenly announced with absolute conviction. 'I got a feeling about this one. I think you're going to see him again real soon.'

Flick smiled a little grimly to herself, wondering what her friend would say if she told her that 'Mr Hot-and-Heavy' was staying in the penthouse suite. She'd deliberately made a point of staying away from the front desk this morning, wanting him to check-out of the hotel without having to face her. If he tried to make contact with her, that was one thing, but she wasn't going to force his hand by encountering him during the course of her job this morning. If he called, it had to be because he wanted to.

'Please let him want to!' she thought as she shooed Jacobina out of her office and turned back to her work. She really liked him. Even now, she could still get that strange excited bubbly feeling just remembering last night.

But it wasn't until the afternoon that she saw him. She glanced up from talking to one of the receptionists and saw him striding across the foyer in a charcoal grey suit that made him look devastatingly attractive. Her stomach did a little jump, and she could feel colour climbing up into her cheeks. She barely noticed that the hotel manager, Leo, was walking beside him.

They approached the front desk, and Flick realised that it would fall to her to deal with whatever the problem was. Pinning on a professional smile, she turned to them.

'Good afternoon, Leo, how can I help you?' She was very careful about not looking at Harrison. Maybe if she had, she'd have had some warning about what was about to come.

'Afternoon, Felicity. I just wanted to make you known to Harrison Lambert. He'll be heading up the renovation project within the hotel for the next six months, so you'll see him coming and going quite a bit.'

Harrison Lambert? Flick blinked, not quite understanding what she was hearing. Her gaze flickered across to Harrison, but he was running an eye across the reception desk, checking on her crew. Then his eyes shifted to lock with hers, and she saw a world full of condemnation and judgement in them. She hadn't misheard that last name, she realised. He was Marc Lambert's brother. Marc Lambert's married older brother.

'When you've got a moment, I'll just get you to switch Harrison's reservation over from Grant to Lambert, thanks,' Leo was saying. 'I think Harrison's done his share of research behind the scenes and is ready to go public.'

Flick could barely nod she was so filled with anger and disgust. He was married. And he was a Lambert. For a moment she thought she might actually be sick. All the horrible memories came flooding back. Her sister screaming at her in the street, disowning her; her terrible flight to Sydney, and the lonely nights in a seedy hotel trying to get her head together. Then the long months of being estranged from her family and judged by friends and neighbours.

'I'll take care of that straight away,' she heard herself say, but it was like hearing an echo down a long tunnel. Her face felt stiff and she realised her smile was frozen in place.

Harrison was still staring at her like she was a bug he'd just squashed with his shoe. Or maybe like a bug he was about to squash with his shoe.

'Right, Harrison, I'll get onto those reports and get them up to the suite in an hour or so,' Leo said. Clapping Harrison on the back, the manager moved off, leaving Flick and Harrison facing each other across the marbled expanse of the reception desk.

Harrison's eyes dropped to the name badge that told the world she was Felicity.

'Flick, Felicity. I should have known when I heard your accent,' he said. His voice was hard.

'I should have known when you offered me that ten dollars,' Flick said, equally cool.

He was married, and he dared to stand there and look at her as though she was the one in the wrong!

Now his eyes were glacier cold as they bored into her.

'I'm putting you on notice, Felicity. Unlike my mother, who allowed herself to be moved by your situation, I have no sympathy for people like you. And I'm not like Marc, unable to see past a pretty face.'

Flick stiffened, flinching at the suppressed fury in his words. He really seemed to despise her. For a moment she felt the sting of tears at the back of her eyes, and then her spine straightened and she thrust her chin out.

'You Lamberts really think you own the world, don't you? Well, you don't scare me. Go back to the penthouse suite and see if you can't buy yourself another girl. But just a tip; you might need to offer a little more than ten dollars for a woman to put up with an arrogant pig like you.'

His face hardened even more, and Flick felt a spurt of fear in her belly. They stood staring at each other, neither willing to cede defeat.

'Flick? You got a moment?' It was Jacobina, phone in one hand, and a couple of impatient looking guests hovering in front of her.

The tension jangled between them for a moment more, and then he flicked his cuff back and checked his watch.

'Don't keep our guests waiting, Ms Scully,' he said imperiously, his face carefully blank and businesslike by the time he looked back at her. 'I'd hate to think you weren't up to the job.'

Flick's hands curled into her palms, but she smiled sweetly.

'Thank you for the advice, Mr Lambert. I'll certainly keep it in mind.'

She turned her back on him then and crossed to deal with Jacobina's situation. By the time she'd dealt with the guests, he'd gone. She was so stunned by what had almost happened between her and Harrison Lambert last night, and what had happened just now, that she simply stood with her palms flat on the cool marble of the desk for a few moments after the guests had gone.

'You doing okay there, Felicity?' Jacobina asked after a while.

Flick pulled herself together and dredged up a smile.

'Absolutely. I'll leave you to it.'

She kept the smile in place until she'd exited into the administrative area behind reception. Gaining her office, she shut the door and sat down behind her desk.

What was she going to do? Harrison Lambert hated her. That was more than obvious. Now that he knew who she was, he had judged her and found her wanting. And he was married!

It made Flick so angry, knowing that he'd tricked her with his false name and his free and easy air. And all the time he had a wife tucked away somewhere. God, she could even remember when they were married. It had been around the same time that Steph and Marc had first met. Marc had been best man at the wedding; she could remember him talking about it. They probably had kids and everything by now.

It made her want to spit, especially when she remembered the feel of him hauling her close last night and kissing her as though he was never going to stop. What a hypocrite! Staring down his nose at her, thinking she was some kind of home-wrecker, when all the time he was the one who was betraying his wife.

And then, of course, there was the fact that he'd threatened her. She was 'on notice', as he'd put it, and she could just imagine what that would entail—Harrison Lambert breathing down her neck every ten seconds, watching and waiting for her to make a mistake. 'I'd hate to think you weren't up to the job.' Those had been his exact words.

Flick stared hard at the wood-grain of her desk, trying to work out what to do. She could ask for a transfer. That would be the smart thing to do, under the circumstances. There were other hotels in the Lassiter's chain, and there were jobs coming up all the time. It would mean difficulties with her work permit, but that wasn't insurmountable.

But even as she thought it, something in her baulked at tucking her tail between her legs and scampering away. She'd done her share of running, she realised. She'd run to Sydney, then she'd come to New York because she couldn't stand the mess she'd made of her sister's life. She'd run enough.

And she'd paid her dues. She'd been left out in the cold by her family, and she'd flagellated herself for months and months over what had happened between her and Marc. Could she have stopped what had happened? Did she encourage him? Had she deliberately set out to steal her sister's happiness the way Steph had said? She'd come out the other side of all that self-doubt thanks to Stuart, and, oddly, thanks to Chloe Lambert for offering her this job in New York.

And she loved her job. She was good at it, too, which was why she'd been promoted recently. And now Harrison Lambert thought he could just stroll in the door and click his fingers and make her disappear, just because she offended his warped sense of family values.

Flick realised that her hands had curled into fists. She wasn't going to go down without a fight, she decided. If Harrison Lambert wanted to get rid of her, she was going to make it damned hard for him. He was going to have to dot all his i's and cross all his t's, or she would make the biggest stink he'd ever seen.

Resolve hardened inside Flick as she pulled her computer keyboard towards herself. 'Bring it on, Harrison Lambert,' she dared him silently. 'I'm ready for you.'

Harrison leaned back in his chair and fiddled idly with the spiral binding on his notepad. The catering manager was talking, discussing the changes in staffing levels and produce that he felt would be required to lift the hotel's catering department up to six star standard. Around him, the heads of the other departments were ranged, all of them diligently taking notes and listening. While his eyes were on the catering manager, Harrison's thoughts were all for the tall, slim blonde seated halfway down the table. He could see her in his peripheral vision. She had her hair fixed in some sort of fancy braid today, and the thick golden plait lay over one shoulder. There was a tiny frown between her eyebrows as she scribbled something on her notepad, and he noticed that she bit her tongue when she was concentrating, just the pink tip of it showing between her lips. On anyone else it would be endearing, charming. On Felicity Scully he found it provocative and highly irritating.

But then, as he'd discovered over the past few days, almost everything she did provoked or irritated him. The cool way she met his eyes when they were forced to interact. The sway of her hips when she walked away from him. The line of her cheek. Her perfume when she passed him in the corridors.

Once, he'd caught her laughing with a colleague, her head thrown back, her laugh loud and unselfconscious. She'd doubled over with laughter, and by the time she registered his presence there were tears in her eyes. The light and laughter had died a quick death when she realised he was watching though. She'd quickly straightened and thrown back her shoulders and given him the cool-eyed stare he was beginning to know very well.

It was that stare that drove him the most crazy, he decided. The presumption in it, the self-assurance. As though he was the one in the wrong. She was just like his soon-to-be-ex-wife, Amanda. She'd looked at him in just the same way when he'd caught her out the front of the hotel that time. No, it had been worse than that. There had been one moment when they first locked eyes when she looked shocked and caught out, and then an expression of resigned impatience had settled over her face. She'd coolly climbed out of the Aston Martin he'd bought her for their last wedding anniversary and sauntered across to him.

'Don't look so shocked, darling. What did you expect?' she'd said.

For a moment he'd been robbed of speech. Who on Earth was this woman? Not the person he'd thought he'd married, that was for sure.

'I don't know, darling,' he'd finally snarled back. 'Fidelity? Love? A bit of honour?'

She'd made a moue of distaste with her glossy lips. 'How very middle class of you. I had no idea you were so pedestrian.'

And he'd almost fallen for it all over again when he met Flick Scully. He could understand why his inexperienced, trusting younger brother had lost his head over Flick. After all, it had almost happened to him, too. If he hadn't known what

Felicity was, he would have bought her act, hook, line and sinker. The thought made his blood boil.

He'd like nothing better than to just march her from the building. Why his mother had seen fit to give her a position within the company was beyond him. Perhaps Chloe had felt some vestige of guilt over the way she'd obstructed Marc's engagement to Stephanie Scully in the first place. Maybe getting rid of Flick was some belated form of recompense. Or perhaps she understood how powerful Flick's hold was over her youngest son, and wanted to remove her from his orbit.

None of it was an excuse for perpetuating her presence in the organisation. And if there weren't labour laws to consider, she'd be gone in a second. Unfortunately, she appeared to be good at her job. She was liked and respected by the rest of the managers, as well as the staff. She worked long hours, she pitched in, and she never complained. He'd since learnt that the reason she was cleaning his suite that first day had been because she was helping out the over-burdened housekeeping department when half the staff had gone down with food poisoning.

His awareness of her flickered as she reached for the water carafe opposite. He noted that she made eye contact with her neighbours to see if they wanted a refill before she poured her own. The small act of politeness made him frown. He'd seen other moments like it over the last few days. Moments that didn't gel with the description of Felicity Scully that first his mother, and then in a drunken, rambling rant Marc had given him. Often she seemed more earnest than cunning, more vulnerable than calculating. He told himself that it was all part of the clever appeal of women like her and Amanda: their apparent sincerity the siren's song luring men to their deaths on the rocks. And it worked, more often than not. After all, he'd bought it enough to marry a woman and stay faithful to her for five years while she cheerfully cuckolded him around the globe.

The catering manager wound up his presentation, and Leo threw the table open to questions. Harrison rolled his pen across his fingers as he listened to a number of astute and not so astute suggestions and questions from the management crew. Then Flick spoke up, and he zeroed in on her like a hawk.

'You mentioned making quite a few changes to the á la carte room service menu,' she said. He noted that she darted a nervous little glance his way, and felt an absurd stab of pleasure. She wasn't completely unaware of him then. 'What about requests that fall outside the menu? What I mean is, our first class guests often like to customise their stays with us. Have you given any thought to that in terms of catering?'

Harrison saw the catering manager shift uncomfortably in his chair; Flick had made a good point. Although most wealthy guests were happy to take what was offered, there were always the select few who wanted to have things their way, to order off the menu. A flexible attitude in the catering department would be needed to accommodate them, but the catering manager had made no mention of it in his presentation.

'The menus we have prepared are extensive. Low carb, low fat, haute cuisine, Atkins, we have something for everyone. I see no reason for guests to want to stray outside the menu offerings,' the catering manager said sniffily.

'Nonetheless, you will make allowance for it,' Harrison said. 'A six star hotel is about service, and service is about flexibility and anticipation.'

The catering manager ducked his head once in submissive agreement, but not before shooting Flick a killer look. She looked uncomfortable. Harrison became aware that she was watching him, her expression unreadable.

'That's all for today,' Leo said, closing his folder. 'We'll meet up again next Thursday to look at the other departments. Felicity, Sadie, you'll both be up then.'

Flick nodded her acceptance of this, apparently unaffected. He watched her stand and leave, his eyes never shifting from her tall, willowy form.

'She's a nice kid, Harrison,' Leo said suddenly from his side.

Harrison turned a frown on the man. 'Meaning?'

'That you should probably not go there unless you're in the market for something serious,' Leo said, holding his eye gamely.

The thought made Harrison snort with derision.

'Having anything with Felicity Scully is the last thing on my mind, trust me,' he said.

Leo just inclined his head in acknow-ledgement, but Harrison noticed with annoyance that he looked unconvinced.

Flick wrote and rewrote the sentence three times before she gave a sigh and let her fingers simply rest on the keyboard of her laptop. She'd been trying to write a review of her department for the past hour, but every time she came up with something she imagined Harrison Lambert's scornful blue gaze boring into her from the other end of the conference room table. He would be gunning for her during her presentation, she knew. Which meant it had to be perfect, absolutely perfect.

He'd surprised her today when he backed her up against the catering manager. It had thrown her for a while, but then she realised that where business was involved he was utterly professional. It was only when it came to her that he appeared to have a blind spot.

Not that she wanted his approval anyway, arrogant pig. All she wanted was for him to finish the refurbishment project and move on. Unfortunately, the end date was almost a full six months away. How was she going to stand this tension for that long? She felt like a clock that had been overwound—any second now and all her cogs and wheels would just pop out all over the place. It was like walking on a highwire and knowing there was no safety net below. She was good at her job, she knew that, but she also knew that things could go wrong, and go wrong very quickly, in the hospitality industry. And she knew as soon as she made a bad decision, or put a foot wrong, Harrison Lambert was going to bring the axe down on her neck.

She'd been pretty careful with money since she'd come to New York. She'd been determined to stand on her own two feet, and even though the rent on her little apartment was pretty steep, and her wages weren't astronomical, she'd been keeping her head above water and even managing to save a little each week. Vaguely in the back of her mind she'd been thinking of a trip home, or maybe shooting across to London for a weekend. But now there was the prospect of losing her job to deal with every day, and the modest balance in her savings account suddenly seemed very meagre. And it wasn't just her she had to worry about now; there was Michelle as well. Having given up her place with her host family, Michelle was completely reliant on Flick finding the rent money every week. It was one thing for Flick to fall over because Harrison Lambert had a taste for revenge, no matter how misplaced, but it was another thing entirely for Michelle's education to suffer.

Thoughts of her sister jogged Flick back to the present. She had to get this presentation done. She needed to push Harrison Lambert out of her mind and just write the report to the best of her ability. She understood how her department worked, and what could be done to improve it. It was simply a matter of putting it all down on paper.

'I'm going to be like a sitting duck when I give this presentation,' she admitted to herself. He was going to sit back with his arms folded and just watch and wait until she said or did something wrong, and then he was going to humiliate her in front of all the other managers. She'd seen him do it to a few others over the past few days, and she knew he had a tongue like a whiplash when he chose to use it. She had no doubt that he would choose to use it on her.

The thought made her feel queasy. No matter how determined she was, no matter what she told herself about being good at her job and having paid for the mistakes of the past, it was impossible to stop the anxiety that was starting to become part of her every day working life.

He'd taken a job she loved and turned it into a battleground. If she hadn't already despised him for sleeping around on his wife, she'd hate him for that. As it was, she had an embarrassment of riches when it came to finding reasons for disliking Harrison Lambert.

The shrill of the phone beside her made Flick start, and she grabbed the receiver on the second ring.

'Flick Scully speaking,' she said, checking the time on the clock on her laptop. It was late, almost midnight.

'Hey, Flick, it's me,' Michelle said. 'Just thought I'd better call and let you know I'm alive and well.'

Flick could tell that something was wrong the moment that Michelle spoke.

'What's wrong, Shell?' she asked, cutting to the chase.

Previously, she and Michelle had never been the closest of sisters, but the past year living in the US together had bonded them. If her sister was hurting, Flick wanted to be able to help.

'It's Connor. Flick, he's got a baby. He slept with Lori when I went to America, and she got pregnant, and she was supposed to have a termination but instead she had the baby,' Michelle blurted, tears in her voice.

For a moment Flick was so stunned she didn't know what to say.

'Jack's Lori, Lori Lee?' she confirmed.

'Yes.' It was a single word, but it was full of a world of misery.

'Shelly ... you must be wrecked. Are they together? Has Connor been lying to you all this time?'

'No. He didn't know. She only just came back to tell him. He's kind of ... freaked out, I guess.'

'No kidding,' Flick thought. She couldn't imagine what it would feel like to suddenly find out you were a parent.

'And where does this leave you?' she asked carefully.

'I don't know. Connor said he still loves me. But I don't know. I'm so angry with him. And Lori. I thought she was my friend.'

Flick thought about what Michelle had said. 'It sounds like it was just one night, though, Shell. It doesn't sound like they love each other or anything.'

'I know. I keep telling myself that.'

They talked for a few more minutes, but Flick was left feeling woefully inadequate when Michelle finally rang off. She simply didn't know what to say. She dropped her head back onto the couch and rubbed her sore eyes. Poor Connor. Poor Lori for that matter. It all just seemed like a great big mess and hardly the idyllic trip home that Michelle had envisaged.

Sighing, Flick lifted her head and opened her eyes and brought her attention back to the laptop screen. She had to get this done, or Harrison Lambert would crucify her. Concentrating fiercely, Flick started typing.

Chapter 4

*F*lick picked up the laser pointer and turned to the projector screen behind her.

' ... as you can see, the figures over the past few months support this. Service levels are up, customer satisfaction has increased. Our market research has shown that more than ninety per cent of our guests would stay with us again.'

The red light from the laser pointer was shaking on the screen, and Flick quickly switched it off. Her hands were shaking. In fact, it felt like her whole body was shaking. No matter what she told herself about being prepared and being able to stand up to anything that Harrison Lambert threw at her, she had been dreading this day.

But she was almost finished, almost across the finishing line. She just had to hang in there.

'So, in conclusion, having an empowered front of office team means that guests will have any problems dealt with on the spot, without having to wait till the manager can be called down or any of the other traditional dispute resolution methods we've used in the past. I firmly believe that a guest with a problem is actually an opportunity for the hotel to step up and exceed his or her expectations,' she said.

She stepped back from the screen, and her colleagues gave her a small round of applause. She deliberately avoided looking towards the end of the table. Harrison had sat through her entire presentation with a closed, impassive expression on his face. Now she could feel his eyes boring into her.

'Any questions?' Leo asked, throwing the discussion open to the table.

'Yes, I have a question for Ms Scully. You're suggesting that we give very junior members of the staff the ability to hand out discounts, order gift baskets and offer vouchers for free accommodation. What makes you think that they're up to this level of responsibility?'

Harrison sounded only idly interested, but she wasn't fooled for a moment. He was going to take a swipe at her. She stiffened her spine, ready to take it on the chin.

'It's a matter of training and mutual respect,' she said. 'I trust my team. They're all very experienced, and they've all shown good judgement in the past.'

Harrison's eyes narrowed. 'So you think that a person's past behaviour is the best way to predict how they're likely to behave in the future? That trustworthy behaviour in the past begets trustworthy behaviour in the future, and vice versa?'

He wasn't talking about her staff, Flick knew. He was saying that because of what had happened with Marc and Steph, she was untrustworthy. For a moment she just stared at him, a thousand thoughts and feelings jostling for position in her mind. She wanted to scream at him to leave her alone. She wanted to tell him that she regretted every second of what happened between her and his brother, that if she could wish it back she would, no matter what it cost her.

But as always with Harrison, her guilt and self-reproach were quickly swamped by righteous anger at his hypocrisy. He was the married guy, sleazing around behind his wife's back, not her. He had no right to sit in judgement of her.

'I think that people make mistakes sometimes, but usually it's unintentional. I'm yet to find an employee who deliberately set out to do wrong,' she finally said.

'I think you're being deliberately naïve, Ms Scully. In my experience, most people know when they're doing something wrong. They simply don't care,' he replied, blue eyes glacial.

'Well, I guess we move in very different circles, Mr Lambert,' Flick fired back.

The rest of the table were following their discussion like spectators at a tennis match, heads swivelling back and forth between them. Aware of the undercurrent, Leo cleared his throat and stepped forward.

'Thanks for that, Felicity. Very comprehensive, and you've certainly thrown up some innovative new ideas for us to consider,' he said.

Flick slid into her seat at the end of the table and gathered her notes into a neat pile. Her hands were still shaking, and she clenched them around her papers. Harrison Lambert was a pig, pure and simple. A pig and a bully, and using his position to threaten her.

The rest of the managers suddenly stood up, and Flick realised that Leo had signed off for the day. Grabbing her papers, Flick shot to her feet and headed for the door. The less time she spent in Mr Pig's company, the better.

She strode towards the lift, smiling as Sadie held the door for her. But as she stepped in and turned to face the doors the smile froze on her face. Harrison Lambert had followed her, and was stepping into the lift beside her. The other managers shuffled to the back to accommodate him, and she tried to angle herself away from him, but it didn't make much difference—she was still standing uncomfortably close to him when the doors slid shut. His aftershave washed over her, something woodsy and tangy. She could see the fine weave of his suit, and the crispness of his shirt. She could even see the faint rise and fall of his chest as he breathed, and feel the heat from his body. She swallowed, realising that her heart was racing all of a sudden.

The lift jerked to a halt on the next floor down, and a number of the managers got out. Flick remembered that there was a training session going on today, she'd already had her session last month. As the doors slid closed again, she took advantage of the extra space to move as far away from him as possible. Eyes trained on the floor indicator, she crossed her arms and waited for this small torturous trip to be over. The lift stopped again, and the last two managers got out. Flick suddenly realised that their departure left her alone with Harrison, and she belatedly made a move to escape. But the doors were already sliding shut, and she was left feeling foolish, fully aware that he knew exactly what was behind her sudden rush forward.

'Don't worry yourself, Ms Scully. I assure you that you're perfectly safe with me. Unlike my brother, I find you completely resistible.'

This brought her head up, and her chin out.

'Don't you ever get sick of reminding the world how important you are?' she threw at him. 'Doesn't it ever get just a little bit old?'

'If you can't stand the heat, Ms Scully ... ' he said, one hand resting casually in the pocket of his pants.

This infuriated Flick, and she spun to face him, her hands clenched into fists by her side.

'You're a real big man, aren't you? Using your power and privilege to bully one of your employees. Yep, you're a real hero,' she said.

He abandoned his casual pose and took a step towards her, brows beetling into a frown as he glared down at her.

'The only reason you're here is because my mother felt some misguided sense of guilt. God knows what tripe you fed her to make her feel sorry for you.'

'I didn't ask your mother for anything. My God, as if I'd want anything from a Lambert. I earned this job, and I earned my promotion, which is more than I can say for you. What's it like going through life knowing that everyone's just tolerating you because you've got money?'

He stepped closer to her now, so that he was looming over her. She refused to back down, tilting her head back to hold his eye and let him know she wasn't afraid of him.

'I know you're used to skating by on your looks, Felicity. But it's not going to work this time. I know exactly what you are, and what you're worth,' he said scathingly.

The ding of the lift arriving in the foyer broke the moment, and Harrison swung away from her and exited. Flick stabbed at the nearest button and sucked in a big lungful of air as soon as he was gone. The lift door closed and she sagged against the wall and tried to blink back the angry tears that were welling in her eyes.

Her hands were shaking again, and she grasped them together and willed them to be still. She would not be intimidated by him. And she would not buy into any of the horrible things he said to her. He didn't know her. All he'd ever heard about her were ugly stories from his mother and brother.

She'd fought so long and hard to forgive herself for what had happened. She had made a mistake, a big one. But that didn't mean he had the right to judge her.

The lift pinged to a halt again and Flick realised she'd sent herself down into the basement car park. She laughed humourlessly— how appropriate. The dark cavernous space was deserted, and she did a few laps, breathing in the cool, slightly damp air and trying to calm herself down. He made her so angry! And the truth was he was really starting to wear her down. After a few weeks of him breathing down her neck, she was beginning to wonder if she could stand a whole six months of this. As much as it galled her, maybe she really should think about asking for a transfer.

But would that solve anything? He would know where she went. She had absolutely no doubt that he had it in for her. He'd just bide his time, and then he'd swoop. So perhaps she should look at another hotel chain. The thought made acid burn in her stomach. She hated the thought of backing down. She'd earned this job, damn him!

Suddenly she remembered the way the Lambert's had looked down their noses when they came to dinner when Marc and Steph had first got engaged. They'd looked around the Scully house as if to say 'is this it?', and they'd poked at their food and they'd done everything they could possibly do to let Steph and her parents know they weren't up to scratch.

Flick punched the button for the foyer. There was no way she was going to let a Lambert chase her out of her job. He could do his worst, and she would endure it. She was a Scully; she could handle it.

Harrison scanned the neatly typed letter

quickly and signed the bottom with an efficiency born of long practice.

'Thank you, Vanessa,' he said, handing the single sheet over to Leo's secretary.

'Not a problem, Mr Lambert,' she said.

'It's Harrison, please. Mr Lambert is my father.'

She smiled her appreciation of this and exited his office, and Harrison went back to studying the interior designer's plans for the new look for the hotel. They were going to upgrade the facilities floor by floor, a process that required careful juggling around of conferences and other peak accommodation periods. Part of his goal was to achieve this as cost and time efficiently as possible. As a result, none of the internal architecture of the rooms would be changing. The bathroom layouts would remain the same, but they would all be updated with new fittings and fixtures. People expected hotel bathrooms to be luxurious, and the new plans promised to live up to that expectation.

The phone to the left of his desk rang, and Harrison reached for it automatically. He was expecting a call from his lawyer to discuss the preliminaries of the divorce.

'Harrison,' a voice purred, and his gut clenched with anger.

'Amanda,' he said coolly, even though she was the last person he wanted to speak to. He wouldn't give her the satisfaction of knowing he cared enough to still get angry with her.

'Darling, I've left several messages. Aren't you talking to me anymore?'

Harrison pulled the receiver away from his ear and stared at it. Was she completely oblivious to the fact that they were getting a divorce?

'Any conversation we need to have can be done through my lawyer, Amanda,' he said shortly, preparing to hang up.

'That's what I wanted to talk to you about, silly,' she said.

Harrison hesitated. 'Meaning?'

'That I think you're taking this man-scorned thing too far. You've moved out, you're working on the other side of the country, point taken. You're angry with me, I understand that. But you don't want to get divorced,' she said silkily.

Harrison raised an eyebrow. He had to hand it to her, his wife was a real piece of work.

'Why not?' he asked bluntly. 'What reason could I possibly have to remain married to you, Amanda?'

'We know each other, Harrison. We understand each other's needs. I know you've had your little affairs on the side over the years. I looked the other way, and I simply expected the same courtesy from you,' she said.

Harrison felt all the empty fury building up inside himself all over again.

'You still don't get it, do you, Amanda. I loved you. There were no little affairs on the side,' he said tightly. 'I mistakenly thought you shared my view of marriage and family. But I've learnt my lesson, thank you.'

He slammed the phone down, and pushed the damn thing as far from him as it could get without falling off the desk. Then he propelled himself out of his chair and crossed to the floor to ceiling window that formed one wall of the office. Raking a hand through his hair, he let out a heavy sigh.

She still had the power to make him angry. He wanted very much to be able to simply look at her and hear her voice and feel nothing at all. He wanted to excise the five years they'd been married from his memory, to just cut it away as though none of it had ever happened.

How long had she been having affairs behind his back? How many years had their marriage been a fraud? It made him feel like an idiot every time he remembered the contemptuous look in her eyes when he'd discovered her that day. How could he have been so mistaken in a person? He'd slept next to her, eaten meals with her, holidayed with her. They'd talked of the future, children. He'd believed in them, in the life they were building together. And it had all been a fantasy—his stupid, naïve fantasy.

For some reason his thoughts turned to Felicity Scully. He remembered how he'd felt that first night with her, as though anything were possible, as though the sky was the limit. And he'd been wrong there, too.

Clearly his judgement couldn't be trusted where women were concerned. Or maybe it was just that all women couldn't be trusted. That was a far better maxim to live by. Much safer. And, in all honesty, he couldn't imagine taking the risk of loving a woman again. How could he ever believe in marriage vows? How could he ever believe that his love was truly returned?

He'd rather be single than a fool. He'd always planned on having children, but he'd leave that up to his siblings now. From now on, it was all about satisfying himself, and that was it. No commitment, no promises, no lies, no betrayals.

⌒

Flick rushed through the crowds of people choking the sidewalk, dodging her way through to the automatic sliding doors into the airport terminal. Her handbag banged against her hip, and she grabbed it with one hand, holding it tight to her body as she dodged through yet more people. She was late, but she was hoping that Michelle's flight had been delayed. As luck would have it, the arrivals display board told her that Michelle's flight from Melbourne had landed early. Flick rushed through to the international arrival area, but there was no sign of Michelle. Craning her neck, Flick tried to see the luggage tags on the people exiting the gate. Were they from Shelly's flight? But the passengers were moving too fast, and Flick finally gave up and approached a burly looking security guard.

'Excuse me, but I don't suppose you know if Flight 181 from Australia has cleared customs yet?' she asked hopefully.

'Yes I do, ma'am. Folks have been coming through for the past half hour or so,' he said.

Flick frowned. Where the hell was Michelle? Then she turned away from the guard and saw a loan figure sitting slumped on a suitcase. It was Michelle, her head drooping down as she stared at the grubby concrete floor. Flick sighed. Poor Michelle. She'd gone home to try and rekindle her first love, and she'd come back more broken-hearted than before.

'Shelly!' she called out, breaking into a jog to cross the last few metres. 'Sorry I'm late. There was a big traffic jam.'

Michelle just looked up at her, her face pale and closed. Flick's heart squeezed in her chest. She knew how it felt to walk away from someone that you loved.

Without saying anything more, Flick slid her arms around her sister and gave her a big hug. Michelle stood stiffly within her embrace, her arms mechanically coming up to hug Flick back. Flick felt tears prick at the back of her eyes. It wasn't until just now that she'd realised how much she'd missed her sister. It had been an awful six weeks. Harrison's persecution had continued at work, and at home she'd sat alone night after night mulling over how empty and unhappy her life had become. Selfishly she'd been looking forward to Michelle's homecoming all week, even though she'd known that Michelle would be coming alone.

'Come on, let's go home,' she said, linking her arm through her sister's and grabbing the suitcase handle.

'I'll take it,' Michelle said, reaching for the case.

'It's okay, I want to do it,' Flick said lightly.

But Michelle just pushed her hands off the grip and started walking towards the taxi rank, the suitcase trailing after her. Flick stared after her for a moment, then hurried to catch up.

'How was the flight? Anything good on the movies?' she asked brightly.

'No.'

'But the flight was okay?' Flick asked again.

Michelle stopped in her tracks and turned to face her.

'Look, I'm really tired, and I really don't want to talk, okay?' she said, not quite meeting Flick's eyes.

Flick flinched at the dead, flat tone in her sister's voice, but forced herself to nod. 'Sure, whatever you want.'

They made the rest of the trip home in silence, and Michelle exited the cab with her luggage without a backward glance. Flick settled the fare and took a deep breath before following her sister up the stairs.

She knew exactly what had happened back home in Erinsborough, of course. Her mother had called her the moment Michelle had gotten on the plane. Despite all Connor's assurances that he still loved her, Michelle had been unable to come to terms with the fact that he was now a father. And, probably more importantly, that he was now linked forever to Lori through the child they'd had together. So Michelle had come back to New York, her first love well and truly a thing of the past now.

The flat felt empty when she entered, and she stuck her head out onto the fire escape with a frown. Where had Michelle gone? Then she heard the sound of running water.

Crossing to the closed bathroom door, she tapped lightly.

'You having a bath, Shelly?' she asked inanely.

Silence greeted her.

'Shelly?' she asked, knocking again.

'What does it sound like I'm doing?' Michelle yelled abruptly.

Flick flinched. She stared at the closed door for a moment then shrugged. Michelle would talk in her own good time.

Michelle pulled her travel-rumpled clothes over her head slowly. She felt awful. Her body felt scratchy and hot, her eyes felt sore, and more than anything she wanted to cry.

But she'd cried too much already. Kicking her clothes into the corner, she climbed into the bath and slid down until the bubbles came up to her chin. The water was hot, almost too hot, and she gritted her teeth until the shock of it passed.

Aunt Valda had advised her to walk away and come back to New York. She'd said that Connor wasn't worth it, that he was untrustworthy and dishonest. But deep down Michelle knew that the real reason she'd left him and come back to New York was because she was a selfish person. She'd left him the first time because she selfishly wanted to go to school in New York, even when she had the best boyfriend in the world at home. Even her jealousy over his night with Lori was because she was selfish—she couldn't stand the thought of anyone else being with him like that. And, worst of all, she was selfish because she didn't want to share him with a baby.

That was the real reason why she'd come back. She didn't want to be some kind of mum to Connor's baby. They had their whole lives ahead of them, the world to explore. And now he had a baby to look after; the biggest responsibility in the world. She understood that he had to look after little Maddy. But she couldn't do it with him. That baby wasn't a part of her the way it was a part of him. And she couldn't stand knowing that from now on she would always come second to him.

Despite her resolve, big fat tears rolled down Michelle's face and into the steaming water. She was so unhappy. There was a big hollow pain inside of her, and she didn't know how it was ever going to go. It was different from when she'd come over the first time. In her heart of hearts, she'd always known she could go back. She'd felt that Connor would wait for her, that their love was special. But now everything had changed. And it would never be the same again.

Michelle stayed in the bath for a long time. When the water was tepid, she pulled the plug and rinsed off under the shower. Then she towelled herself dry and padded out into the living area. Flick was curled up on the couch reading a magazine. She smiled tentatively, but Michelle didn't want her sister's sympathy.

Zipping her suitcase open, Michelle dragged on a skirt and top and slid her feet into some shoes. Crossing back to the bathroom, she wiped the steam from the mirror and quickly plaited her hair into a presentable style. A quick wave of the mascara wand and a touch of lipstick, and she figured she could pass okay. Trailing back to her suitcase, she pulled out her jacket and picked up her purse.

Flick looked surprised when she saw her sling the purse strap over her shoulder.

'Are you going out?' she asked.

'Yep,' Michelle said. She couldn't stand the idea of being alone with her own thoughts. She wanted to get out, do something, distract herself from the empty feeling inside.

'Where?'

'Don't know, don't care,' Michelle said, pulling the front door open.

Flick was standing, heading towards the door, her face puckered into a frown.

'Shelly ...' she said, but Michelle just pulled the door shut between them and started down the stairs.

She heard the door open behind her, and she could feel Flick watching her down the stairwell. Her shoulders relaxed when she finally heard the door to the apartment shut again. Good. She didn't want Flick hanging around being nice to her. She didn't deserve it.

She was pushing her way through the double doors and out into the street when she ran into the baking guy from apartment one.

'Michelle Scully,' he said instantly.

Michelle frowned at him, barely able to remember his name.

'Oh, hi,' she said diffidently. She didn't want to stop and chat.

'You've been away,' he said brightly, hands tucked into the back pockets of his jeans.

He wasn't dressed for work today, she realised belatedly. Instead, he was wearing black denim jeans and a faded red T-shirt. He looked happy and relaxed, totally at peace with the world.

'Yeah. I went home for a while.'

'Yeah? Did you have a good time?' he asked.

He was smiling down at her, and suddenly all Michelle wanted to do was scream at him. Why couldn't everybody mind their own business?

'I've got to go,' she said, pushing past him rudely.

She didn't look back as she made her way up the street. All she wanted was to be left alone.

Flick glanced at the clock on the wall again and ran a hand across her forehead. She had a tension headache, and guessed vaguely that she should take some tablets. But she knew the best cure would be for Michelle to come home.

It was two in the morning, and she hadn't heard a word from Michelle since she'd slammed out of the house that afternoon. At first she'd expected her home for dinner, but as time wore on, she began to worry. Michelle had seemed so angry and sad. She should have insisted that she stay and talk, rather then just let her stalk off like that.

As time passed, Flick alternated between feeling a stomach-churning fear for her sister, and being overcome with anger that Michelle would put her through this. One of the discussions they'd had when Michelle began her campaign to get Flick to let her move in had been about curfew. Flick had not been keen to take on the role of Michelle's guardian and disciplinarian, but Michelle had assured her that she wouldn't be any trouble. Between the two of them they had roughed out some guidelines. Michelle had promised to never be home later than midnight, and if she were going to be any later, she would always call.

It was easy to get carried away with fear in New York. The newspapers were full of murders and rapes and shootings and muggings. Flick had never had a problem the whole time she'd been here, but she'd heard things through the people at work. This was a big, crowded city, and bad things happened. It wasn't like Erinsborough, where you could pretty much do anything at anytime and know that you'd be safe. Here, neighbours didn't look out for each other or invite each other over for barbeques.

Flick chewed on a fingernail and wondered if she should call home. But what would she say? 'Hi, Mum, I seem to have lost my sister'? She'd only upset Lyn, and there was nothing her mum could do from the other side of the world anyway. Wrapping her arms around her torso, Flick paced to the window and peered down into the street. Everything was silent and dark down below.

Maybe she should try the hospitals. The thought made her feel sick, and she suddenly felt very alone. For some absurd, insane reason, she wished that Harrison Lambert were there right now. He'd know what to do. He always seemed to know what to do, and she could use some of his arrogant self-assurance right about now.

Before she could register exactly how aberrant and bizarre the idea of leaning on Harrison Lambert was there was a knock on the door. Relief surging through her, Flick raced across to open it, flinging the door open without even checking who was on the other side.

It was Michelle, thank God, with some guy who looked vaguely familiar. Michelle was bleary-eyed and staggering, and the guy was supporting her. Flick smelt the malty odour of beer and realised that her sister was drunk.

'I found her downstairs. I think she was a bit lost,' the guy said.

Flushing with embarrassment and concern for her sister, Flick moved to take Michelle's weight off him.

'I'm really sorry. Thanks for bringing her up here,' she said.

'It's okay. We've all been under the weather before,' he said, helping Flick guide Michelle over to the couch.

Michelle slumped onto the cushions with a low groan, and Flick had a fair idea that her sister was going to be very embarrassed about this tomorrow.

Flick turned to Michelle's rescuer and stuck her hand out.

'I'm Flick, Michelle's sister,' she said. 'Are you one of Michelle's friends from school or something?'

'Charlie McKenzie,' he said, shaking her hand firmly. 'I live downstairs in number one. I met Michelle the other day.'

He glanced down at Michelle when he said her name, and there was a certain light in his eye. Flick raised an eyebrow; it looked like her sister had made a conquest, and she hadn't even been in the building a month.

'Charlie, you're a life saver. We owe you one,' she said.

He waved a hand dismissively. 'Like I said, it's no big deal.'

Nodding his head goodbye, he let himself out. Flick turned and considered her sister.

'Michelle, what on Earth were you thinking?' she finally asked.

Michelle just closed her eyes and turned her face away.

'You want to tell me how you got this drunk?' Flick demanded. But she knew it was futile—Michelle was as drunk as a skunk.

Crossing to the kitchen, Flick poured a big glass of water and brought it into the lounge.

'Here, you'd better try to drink this,' she said.

Michelle took one look at the glass, and a strange look passed across her face. Flick stepped back just in time as Michelle launched herself towards the bathroom. She winced as she heard Michelle retch into the toilet. At least she hoped it was the toilet. Putting the glass of water carefully beside the fold-out bed, she padded into the bathroom to find Michelle slumped against the bathroom wall, her face pale.

'Feeling any better?' she asked.

In answer, Michelle just reached for the toilet bowl again.

It was a long night. Flick spent most of it trying to ease Michelle's self-inflicted suffering. By the time her alarm went off in the morning she'd only managed a few hours sleep and she went into work with gritty eyes and a slow brain.

As fate would have it, it was a long, gruelling day. Harrison handed out the schedule for the renovations, and she quickly realised that it was going to require some careful juggling of the reservations in the upcoming months. Each week there would be hotspots for construction noise, and her and her team would have to try to shuffle guests around them on the floors above and below to try and ensure no one would be inconvenienced by the racket. With the work commencing the following week, Flick spent the entire morning drawing up a series of plans for her reference so she could keep a running track of where the construction teams would be every day.

While she was at it, she taped a clean yearly planner to her wall and circled the renovation end date in bold red pen. She looked at the date a little longingly. Not only would it mark the hotel's ascension to six stars, it would also mean good riddance to Harrison Lambert. 'Bring it on,' she thought ruefully.

'Practicing a bit of voodoo, Ms Scully?'

Flick grit her teeth and turned her coolest smile on the tall, arrogant length of man filling her office doorway.

'Whatever it takes, Mr Lambert,' she said.

'Is that a personal credo?' he asked, lounging against the doorframe.

'Just a survival technique. Was there something I could help you with?' she asked pointedly.

As usual when she was in his presence, her heart had kicked up a gear and she could feel her pulse thrumming in her ears.

'I need to know what arrangements have been made to accommodate the renovation schedule,' he asked, straightening abruptly from his position near the door.

Flick unrolled the large-format copies she'd made of each of the hotel's floor plans.

'We're going to track the construction daily to ensure guest comfort,' she explained stiffly, indicating the timelines, and flipping through the plans to show how the hotel bookings would alter on at least a weekly basis.

The hard planes of his face were unreadable as he perused the plans, then his eyes flicked up to her face.

'This is a good idea. Who came up with it?' he asked.

Flick felt herself blush. 'I did,' she said, waiting for him to retract his praise or undercut it in some way.

But he didn't. He just ducked his head slightly in acknowledgement.

'Good work.'

For a moment they just stood there, the silence stretching between them. Flick was terribly aware of every inch of him, of the way his dark navy suit jacket was unbuttoned, displaying the flatness of his belly, and the way the hair curled over his ears and around to the nape of his neck. She could smell his aftershave—different from the other day—and see the shadow of his beard beginning to grow, even though he'd only shaved a few hours ago.

His eyes scanned her face, almost as though he was looking for something. Then he simply turned on his heel and exited her office without saying another word.

She felt like a piece of over-cooked spaghetti, and she sagged against her desk. Why did she let him affect her like this?

She still didn't have a decent answer by the time she trudged up the last flight of stairs to the apartment that night. She was late, having been held up at work, and she'd bought takeaway on the way home to make it up to Michelle. If her sister were anything like her, she'd have been craving junk food today.

But Michelle was in the bathroom when she got in, putting the finishing touches on her make-up. Flick eyed the slinky black dress her sister was wearing with dismay.

'Haven't got time for dinner,' Michelle said when she smelt the Indian food. 'The girls are meeting me downstairs in five minutes.'

'Michelle, you're not going out again tonight. You're back to school again tomorrow.'

'I'll be there, take a chill pill,' Michelle said, adjusting her hair minutely.

She brushed past Flick on her way through to the living room, and Flick noticed with annoyance that her sister had helped herself to her one bottle of good perfume.

'Michelle, I don't want you to go out again. In fact, I think we should talk about what happened last night,' Flick said.

There was the sound of a car horn beeping in the street outside, and Michelle stuck her head out the window.

'Coming!' she hollered out the window, then grabbed a light jacket and her purse and made for the door.

'Michelle! Stop and at least tell me where you're going, please,' Flick demanded, hating that she sounded exactly like their mother.

'Out,' Michelle said succinctly. 'And don't bother waiting up for me.'

Chapter 5

*M*ichelle stood with her back to the wall, a plastic cup of beer in one hand. Music pumped loudly, and smoke coiled lazily near the ceiling. All around her, kids were talking and dancing and kissing and smoking and drinking. And Michelle felt as isolated and alone as if she was standing in the middle of a desert.

Her school friends Madison and Chantelle were working it on the makeshift dance floor, showing off moves they'd learnt from music videos. They'd given up on getting Michelle to come and join them long ago, leaving her to her dark thoughts.

Michelle swallowed the last of the lukewarm beer in her cup and pushed herself away from the wall. The keg was in the kitchen. She just had to remember where that was. The floor seemed to lurch up at her as she tried to pick her way past a couple locked together near the couch. She staggered, grabbing at the coffee table for balance. Someone laughed at her, and she forced a half-hearted smile back, just to show that everything was cool.

But everything was far from cool. She was stuck here in New York, and for the first time since she'd arrived she didn't want to be here. But she didn't want to go home, either. The truth was, she didn't know where she wanted to be, or even who she wanted to be anymore. She hated being Michelle Scully, couldn't stand looking at herself in the bathroom mirror every morning. She'd ruined everything. She'd walked away from Connor when she still loved him, and now she'd gotten her just desserts. Whenever she closed her eyes to picture him, she saw the look on his face when he held baby Maddy in his arms. That was the only way she could remember him now.

And she was so sick of thinking all this stuff over and over. Nothing changed. She never had an amazing insight that suddenly made everything make sense. She didn't feel any better. She just hurt. And she couldn't seem to stop it.

One hand on the wall for balance, Michelle walked carefully up the hall. A doorway opened on her left, and she sighed with relief when she saw it was the kitchen. The big silver keg still sat on the kitchen bench, and she filled her cup up to the brim.

'All right, party girl,' a guy said nearby.

He was tall and skinny, and he smiled at her speculatively. Michelle gave him a dirty look.

'In your dreams, pal,' she said, the words slurring slightly as she turned back into the hallway.

'Like I was interested anyway,' he called after her.

She must have turned the wrong way, away from the living room and towards the bedrooms, because suddenly there was a big bed in front of her. She couldn't even remember whose apartment this was. It didn't matter. There were so many kids at her school there was always something happening.

The bed was occupied, she realised. A boy and a girl, rolling around, not caring that the door was open and that anyone could see what was going on. Michelle retreated, shutting the door behind her. She was in the hall again now, and she stared back along the length of it towards the lighted square that was the doorway to the living room. She could hear the music and the laughter, but none of it mattered. Her back to the wall, Michelle slid down until she was sitting on the ground. She swallowed the last half-cup of beer in one gulp, then put her head back. She just wanted to stop feeling. If she got drunk enough, sometimes the pain went away. Sometimes it got worse, too. But she didn't know what else to do at the moment.

She realised she was crying, the salty taste of tears running down the back of her throat. She let them fall. It didn't matter. None of it mattered.

She woke up to find Madison standing over her, nudging her with the toe of her shoe.

'Hey, Michelle, we're going,' she said.

Michelle tried to sit up straighter, but her back complained and she realised she'd fallen asleep hunched over against the wall. Her face felt stiff from the tears, and she blinked her eyes blearily.

'Won't be a moment,' she promised, rolling onto her side and pushing herself laboriously to her feet. The world span a little but quickly settled; she must have been asleep for some time.

'Girlfriend, you are wasted,' Chantelle said as they made their way out of the apartment and waited for the lift.

'I'm fine,' Michelle assured her.

Chantelle and Madison exchanged knowing looks. 'If you say so.'

Michelle stared out the window of the cab as it took them home. Chantelle and Madison were discussing the party, who got with whom, who broke up, who said what. But Michelle couldn't be bothered with any of it. When the cab got to her place she just handed over her share of the fare and staggered out of the car.

'See you tomorrow, Shelly,' Chantelle called as the cab motored off.

Michelle waved a hand, then turned and stared up at the apartment building. The light was on in their place, and she guessed Flick was up waiting for her again. The last thing she wanted was a lecture from her sister.

Realising it was unavoidable Michelle dug her keys out of her purse and let herself into the foyer. She had crossed to the bottom of the first flight of stairs when she registered the strip of light leaking beneath the door to apartment number one. Faint music drifted out into the foyer, and Michelle shrugged to herself and wandered across to tap on the door.

A few seconds later the door swung open, and Charlie was standing there, his hair standing on end as though he'd been running his hands through it. He was wearing a black singlet and a pair of worn jeans, and he looked tired.

'Michelle,' he said, ducking his head out of his doorway and looking around to see if anyone else was with her.

'It's just me. Wanted to say thanks for last week, when you took me upstairs,' she said. Her voice slurred a little on the last word, and Charlie frowned.

'Have you been drinking again?' he asked.

'Does it matter?' she asked.

Charlie ran his hand through his hair. 'I think you should go home, Michelle,' he said, starting to swing the door shut.

Michelle instinctively put her foot in the way so that it wouldn't close. She didn't want to go upstairs. Even if she didn't have a fight with Flick, it would take ages for her to get to sleep and she didn't want to lie in bed and think about Connor for hours.

'Please. Couldn't I just come in for a little while?' she cajoled.

Charlie stared at her for a long moment. 'Please?'she repeated,sensing he was weakening.

He shrugged and stepped away from the door, and she moved past him into his apartment.

It was roughly the same size as Flick's, but designed slightly differently. The kitchen was open plan, not in a separate space, and she saw that Charlie had lots of shiny cookware and utensils. The wall of the living area was dominated by a huge bookcase loaded with cookbooks and novels and a big old lumpy sofa filled one corner. Because his windows looked out onto the street, the glass was frosted and he hadn't bothered to close the blinds.

'Have you just finished work?' she asked, dropping her bag on the kitchen bench.

'An hour or so ago. Haven't you got school tomorrow?' he asked, crossing to the sink to put the kettle on.

Michelle pulled a face. 'Doesn't matter. I'm passing okay.'

'Just passing. Right,' he said as he spooned instant coffee into a cup.

'What's that supposed to mean?' she asked, piqued by his dismissive tone.

'Nothing. I s'pose I thought you were a bit smarter than that,' he shrugged.

'It's just high school. It doesn't mean anything,' she found herself saying.

'There's an attitude that'll take you places.'

Michelle glared at him as he slid a cup of black coffee in front of her.

'Whether I pass school or not is nothing to do with you, if you don't mind,' she said.

'You're the one who came knocking on my door, Michelle. You're the one I had to help up four flights of stairs because she was too out of it to make it on her own the other night.'

Michelle shoved the coffee cup back at him. 'Look, I just saw your light on and thought you might be up. It doesn't give you the right to tell me what to do. I get enough of that from my sister.'

'She's probably worried about you. You're too young to be writing yourself off like this,' he said.

Michelle snatched up her handbag. 'Thanks for the lecture. It was great,' she said as she wrenched the front door open.

He just stood by the kitchen bench and watched as she slammed the door shut behind her. Thoroughly incensed, Michelle stalked the four flights up to the apartment. Where did he get off, standing there giving her advice like he was her big brother or something? He'd helped her out once, that was all.

The light was on in Flick's bedroom, and she came and stood in the doorway as Michelle threw her clothes off and dragged her pyjamas on.

'It's nearly three o'clock, Michelle,' she said flatly.

'And?'

Michelle tossed the cushions off the couch and pulled the bar that activated the bed mechanism. The bed unfolded with a metallic groan, and Michelle climbed into it and deliberately switched off the light. She could feel Flick standing in the dark for a few minutes, just watching her. She concentrated on making her breathing deep and even, as though she had fallen asleep on the spot.

'You're not fooling anyone, Shelly. We're going to talk about this tomorrow, or you can find yourself somewhere else to live,' Flick said quietly.

Michelle heard the scuff of her sister's bare feet on the floorboards, and then the soft click of the bedroom door closing. Eyes flicking open, she rolled over onto her back and stared at the ceiling. The beer was wearing off now, and the emptiness inside her seemed to stretch on forever.

'I love you, Connor,' she told the ceiling.

Then she turned her face into the pillow to muffle her crying.

Flick had set the alarm to wake her an hour ahead of her normal time, and as soon as it went off she padded straight out into the living room. Michelle was sprawled on her stomach, her face creased into an anxious expression even though she was asleep. The smell of alcohol hung heavily in the air, and Flick crossed to the window and pushed it all the way up, letting the fresh morning air in.

'Michelle,' she said, giving her sister's shoulder a shake. 'It's time to get up, Michelle.'

Michelle grunted and screwed up her face,

trying to push Flick's hand away. Flick ignored her protests and shook her again.

'Come on. Up. I'm going to have a shower, and when I come out, we're going to talk,' she said.

Michelle's eyes flickered open, and a mutinous expression crossed her face.

'I mean it, Shelly,' Flick said.

She left Michelle to finish waking up on her own and headed into the shower. Five minutes later, she tied the sash on her dressing gown and headed back out into the living room. Michelle was sitting up in bed nursing a mug of coffee.

'I made you some,' she said, indicating a cup on the side table.

Flick smiled faintly, well aware that Michelle was laying the groundwork for some major sucking up. It was a technique they'd both used with their mother over the years.

'Thanks. But it's not going to change what I'm going to say,' Flick said. 'Michelle, we can't go on like this. We made a deal when you moved in. Remember? I don't want to be your keeper.'

'Then don't be. I'm old enough to take care of myself. I'm doing okay at school. I don't see what the big deal is,' Michelle said.

'The big deal is that you are doing everything you can to hurt yourself,' Flick said.

Michelle made a rude noise and rolled her eyes.

'You are, Shelly. What do you call writing yourself off every night? Do you have any idea how bad binge drinking is for you?'

'Don't pretend you didn't do it when you were my age,' Michelle sniffed.

'I won't. Absolutely I got tanked a few times—but I was at home, with friends my own age, and I didn't do it every night of the week. You're supposed to be here to learn, Michelle, not to party hard with college-age kids at keg parties.'

'I'm fine. I can take care of myself.'

'Right. Which is why the nice guy from downstairs had to bring you home last week.'

They just stared at each other.

'If you want to talk, I'm here,' Flick finally said. 'But I don't want you living here if you're going to keep carrying on like this. I love you, Shelly, and if you won't let me help you you're going to have to go home, or go back to the Roland's. I won't sit by while you stuff up your life.'

Michelle swore under her breath and kicked the covers off her feet angrily.

'This is such a load of crap. I'm not doing drugs or sleeping around or anything, I'm just having a bit of fun. Is that suddenly against the law now?'

Flick just crossed her arms and held her sister's eye.

'It's your choice, Shelly,' she said, turning on her heel and heading into her room to get dressed for work.

Flick could hear Michelle stomping around in the living room and kitchen as she did her hair and pulled on her clothes. She was really worried about her sister. Michelle had always been quiet and studious, the serious one of the family. When she got a bee in her bonnet about something, she was unstoppable. Animal rights, vegetarianism, you name it, if Michelle felt strongly, she'd fire up and make a fuss. Now it felt like she was channelling all that focus and energy into hurting herself. Flick had tried over and over again to get her to talk about Connor and what had happened back home, but Michelle hadn't said a word about any of it. Instead, she'd just gone out every night, returning home later and later each time, stinking of beer and spirits.

Flick hated having to give an ultimatum like this, but she was at her wits end. She couldn't forbid Michelle from going out, or police her activities when she did. They were sisters, not mother and daughter. But she couldn't sit back and watch and wait for something bad to happen, either. This was her last shot at getting Michelle to wake up and see what she was doing to herself.

Silence greeted her when she exited her room, ready to head into work. Michelle was folding up the bed, but Flick noted that she'd pulled the linen and blankets off the mattress before stowing it. She frowned. Then she saw that Michelle had started packing all her clothes back into her suitcase.

'What's going on, Shelly?' Flick asked warily.

'I'm going. What does it look like? I know when I'm not wanted.'

Flick sighed. 'That's not what I said, and you know it.'

Michelle ignored this, and just kept reassembling the sofa.

'Where are you going to go, then?' Flick asked, trying another tact.

'Like you care.'

'I do care, Michelle. That's why I'm doing this,' Flick pointed out.

Suddenly Michelle rounded on her, angrily flinging one of the couch cushions onto the floor.

'What would you know? You just walk around in your perfect little world, doing whatever Miss Felicity wants. You click your fingers and things just fall into your lap. You want Steph's fiancé? Bam—he's yours. You want Stuart? Suddenly you're engaged. You want a sexy job in New York? Why not, whatever Princess Flick wants. When has anything ever gone wrong in your life, Flick?' Michelle hissed; her eyes narrowed with fury.

Flick took a step back from her sister's

venom, stung despite herself. She knew Michelle was hurt and lashing out, but that didn't mean her words didn't hit home. Michelle had always had this view that she was some sort of untouched princess, picking her way through life like it was a field of flowers. Remembering the past two months of hell with Harrison Lambert breathing down her neck, and the pain of what had happened over Marc and Steph, and the hurt of breaking things off with Stuart, Flick almost found it in herself to laugh at her sister's misapprehension.

Almost, but not quite.

Instead, she drew herself up a little straighter and shouldered her backpack.

'I have to go,' she said.

Michelle didn't say another word as she left the apartment and started down the four flights of stairs. Flick blinked furiously. She would not cry because her sister said something nasty in a fight. They weren't kids anymore, and it didn't matter what Michelle thought of her.

Except that she'd thought the two of them had become friends over the past year or so, the two Scully sisters facing the big city together. Obviously she'd been wrong.

Her head was still full of the problems with Michelle when she arrived at work, but the tangle of people crowding the reception desk told her that she was going to have to put all that to one side—unless she was very much mistaken, there was trouble brewing. Suitcases were stacked haphazardly all over the place, and clumps of disgruntled looking people clotted the foyer. When Jacobina glanced up and caught her eye, her gut feeling was confirmed.

Giving the concierge a quick smile, she asked him to mind her backpack so she could go straight to Jacobina's rescue. Then, pinning a smile in place, she crossed the foyer to the front desk.

'Good morning, how's everything going here?' she asked.

Jacobina quickly filled her in on the situation: one of the many independent Internet travel web sites that funnelled bookings through to the hotel had had some sort of glitch with their bookings system. As a result, there were two tour buses full of tired tourists wanting to check into their rooms, but the hotel had no reservations for them. Jacobina was madly trying to accommodate them all, but with a whole floor out of action due to the renovations, it was looking difficult, if not impossible.

Flick called up the reservations program and had a look at what was available. As Jacobina had already worked out, there just weren't enough rooms. Frowning, Flick considered the floor marked off for renovations. The work crews had only moved in last week. How far had they gone in that time?

Her stomach knotted with tension as she realised who could answer that question for her. Reaching for the phone, she dialled Harrison's office. He answered on the second ring.

'Harrison Lambert,' his deep voice said into her ear.

Flick swallowed a lump of nervousness. 'Harrison, it's Felicity Scully on reception. We have a situation here. There's been a software issue with one of our accommodation on-sellers, and we have two tour buses of guests that we have no reservations for. I've just taken a look at room availability, but the only way we can accommodate them all is if we take back some of the rooms from the renovation floor. What's the state of play with those rooms?'

There was a long pause, and she pictured Harrison's face becoming intent and focused as he processed their dilemma. She heard the rustle of papers.

'More than half of the floor has been stripped bare,' he said, 'and the work crews are already into the other half of the rooms as we speak.'

'Can we stop them? Or should I put a call out to Lassiter's Plaza downtown?' Flick asked.

In an absolute emergency, they could try to palm off some guests onto one of their sister hotels, but it wasn't the preferable option. The other hotel was way across town, and they'd have to offer major discounts to soothe the unhappy guests who got shunted there.

'Let me make a call.'

And then she was listening to the dial tone. Thinking quickly, she made a quick internal call to warn the catering staff of her intentions then she replaced the handset and turned to the assembled throng of impatient tourists.

'Ladies and gentlemen, we are attempting to solve this problem for you. I hope that I will have your accommodation requirements sorted in the near future, but in the meantime I'd like to invite you all to take some complimentary morning tea in our hotel restaurant.'

Flick walked out from behind the desk and gestured towards the entrance to the restaurant. People complained, of course. As Flick circulated the foyer and passed her message onto each glut of guests, there were a number of people who stepped up to complain bitterly about being tired, hungry, needing a shower, and wanting their room—which, they assured her, had already been paid for in advance. Flick smiled through it all, promised the problem would be resolved in the shortest possible time, and urged them to take some refreshment in the hotel restaurant.

By the time all the bus groups had filtered through to the restaurant, Flick turned to find Harrison waiting by the front desk.

'How did we go?' she asked, holding her breath.

'I think we can do it. It'll mean sending the work crews home for the day, but these guys are only overnighters, right?'

'That's right. Do you have a list of room availability on that floor?'

Harrison handed across a sheet, and she flashed him a grateful glance, he was one step ahead of her already.

'What do you want me to do? Go in and get details from the guests? Do it table by table?' Jacobina asked.

With no booking details, each guest was going to have to be checked in from scratch, a time consuming procedure, and one that was bound to incite even more complaints and impatience from their guests. Flick frowned, thinking fast.

'What was the name of the on-seller web site that fell over on all this?' she asked.

Jacobina pushed a printed confirmation sheet across the desk to Flick. Very aware of Harrison watching their every move, Flick made her decision.

'I'm going to call these people, see if I can't get a download or faxed list of the bookings. At the very least it will mean we can book guests in without disturbing their morning tea, and only call them out from the restaurant when their rooms are ready,' she said.

She flicked a glance across at Harrison. His expression was unreadable, and she reached for the phone. Five minutes later, she pulled a long list of booking details from the fax machine.

'Let's get stuck in,' Flick said to Jacobina.

She'd already called up two other girls from administration who she knew had experience on the hotel's reservation software, and she divided the list up so that Jacobina, the two girls and herself could tackle the bookings simultaneously.

'Here, give me some of that,' Harrison said. He held out a hand imperiously. 'There are five consoles here, I can input some of the bookings.'

Flick stared at him, genuinely stunned.

'Don't look so surprised, Ms Scully Believe it or not, I worked as a reception clerk for some time. I'm familiar with the software,' he said.

Flick dutifully tore off a section of the list, and handed it over. His fingers brushed against hers for the briefest of moments as he took the paper from her hands, and she snatched hers back reflexively, turning away to hide her reaction.

It was the first time they had touched since finding out the truth about one another, and it disturbed her to realise that on some level she still found him attractive. Forcing the issue to the back of her mind, she reached for the keyboard. As if this task hadn't been stressful and demanding enough, now she had to perform it with her nemesis seated beside her. Gritting her teeth, Flick set to with a vengeance.

Michelle stormed around the house after Flick had gone, anger fuelling her as she packed. How dare Flick stand there and judge her! She so wasn't into a position to judge anyone. How Michelle dealt with her problems was her choice, not Flick's. It was her business, and she didn't see what it had to do with her sister at all. And now Flick was kicking her out because she'd gone out a few times. Big deal. Just because Flick had no life of her own here in New York.

Guilt stabbed at Michelle as she remembered the hurt look in her sister's eyes when she'd yelled at her. In her heart, she knew that Flick had had her fair share of pain and suffering. She knew how heartbroken and messed up she'd been over all that mess with Marc and Steph. But it didn't mean that Flick understood what Michelle was going through, or give her the right to tell her what to do. She'd been living in New York for well over a year. She knew how to take care of herself.

It wasn't until she had stuffed the last of her things into her case and sat on it to zip it closed that Michelle realised she had nowhere to go. She could call Chantelle or Madison, of course, but that would only be a temporary solution. For a second she toyed with the idea of making contact with the Rolands in Jersey. But they'd been hurt and a little offended when she'd told them she was moving in with her sister. And the thought of going back to the quiet suburbia of Jersey just made her angry all over again.

She had nowhere to go, and no one understood her, and she was so miserable she felt like she could throw up with it. She wanted to cry but no tears would come, and she wanted to smash something but everything around her was Flick's and she wasn't the sort of person who did stuff like that, anyway. Most of all she wanted to call Australia and beg Connor to forgive her and please try to make it work. But she knew she could never do that, because she didn't have the courage to take on being a mother to Maddy.

Michelle's head ached from last night and her fight with Flick. She angrily stormed into the bathroom to have a shower and try to calm down.

Three hours after walking in the door for work, Flick pushed some stray strands of hair off her forehead and stepped back from the bookings console. Her shoulders ached from hunching over the machine for so long, and she rolled them to ease the pain.

'That, I think, is that,' she announced.

For the past few hours the five of them had worked at full bore to input data and assign rooms for nearly one hundred and fifty guests. One of the porters had been conscripted to ferry guests from the restaurant across to the reception desk as reservations were finalised, and slowly but surely the crowd in the restaurant had dwindled down to nothing. Every room in the hotel was booked, the restaurant had served innumerable cups of complimentary tea and coffee, but the guests were, at last, in their rooms and satisfied.

Jacobina pumped a fist in the air and did a quick jig. 'Whoo-hooo!' she said.

Flick smiled, but she was all too aware of the fact that Harrison Lambert had been an ever-present witness during their crisis. Bracing herself, she turned to thank him for his help.

He'd taken off his jacket and rolled up his sleeves sometime over the past few hours. Periodically she'd caught a whiff of his aftershave as he worked beside her, but she'd refused point blank to look at him. She felt like a piece of piano wire, stretched taut enough to break. The pressure of accommodating so many unexpected guests was challenge enough, but doing it under the critical eye of a man who had her in his sights had been a peculiar form of torture. Every fumble of the keyboard, every misstep, every hesitation— she felt as though he had been judging her every move, just waiting for a mistake big enough to send her packing.

But now they were done, and he could go back to his office, and she could get on with her job. The crisis was over. Of course, he might still choose to criticise her handling of the situation. But for the moment she just wanted him gone.

'Thank you for your assistance, Harrison, but I think we can take it from here,' she said, forcing a smile that she hoped looked grateful and confident.

He didn't respond, just kept tapping away, finalising his last booking. She couldn't help noticing that he'd loosened his tie and unbuttoned the top of his shirt, and that now a small triangle of his chest was visible. It looked tanned and well muscled. She flickered her eyes back up to Harrison's face, only to find he was watching her intently now. Feeling thoroughly exposed, Flick felt embarrassed heat climbing her cheeks. And still he watched, taking everything in, studying her in almost the same way that she'd been studying him. Suddenly she was aware that she'd chewed her lipstick off ages ago, that her hair had come loose from its neat French roll and strands were now framing her face, and that she had also taken her blazer off and was down to her shirtsleeves.

'Felicity, there's a call for you,' Jacobina said, her voice breaking the moment.

Flick reached for the phone gratefully, but soon realised this was the last call she wanted to receive.

'Felicity?' a male voice asked.

'Speaking. How can I help you?' she responded professionally.

'My name's Charlie McKenzie, we met the other night when I brought Michelle upstairs. I don't want to alarm you, but I was up visiting the Lee's in the apartment beneath yours just now and I heard a big thump from your place. Really big, like someone falling over or something, you know? So I went up and knocked on your door, but no one answered. You wouldn't happen to know if Michelle was home, would you?'

A cold finger of fear ran up Flick's spine. Michelle could still have been home, she knew.

'You don't have a spare key with anyone in the building, do you?' Charlie was asking. 'I thought I could just check that everything's all right for you.'

Flick tried to suppress the many fearful thoughts clamouring for attention in her mind.

'Umm, Mr Mustaffa, opposite the Lee's. We swapped keys a few months ago,' Flick said.

'Okay. I'm going to pop across and see if he's in. Do you want me to call you back or do you want to wait?' Charlie asked.

'I'll wait,' Flick said. It was stupid, but she

felt like she was more connected to the situation if the line was open, even if it was just an illusion.

She heard Charlie put the phone down and she turned away from Jacobina's concerned face. Harrison was still sitting at the console next to hers, and she put her hand up to shield herself from him. All the while she was thinking of Michelle. 'Please let her be all right, please let her be all right.'

After what seemed like too short a time Charlie was back. He was out of breath, and panic blossomed in her belly as soon as she heard the urgency in his voice.

'Felicity, I've found Michelle. She seems to have fallen getting into the bathtub. She's unconscious, and I've called an ambulance,' he said tightly.

Flick gripped the phone receiver as though her life depended on it.

'But she's breathing, right? She's alive?' she demanded.

'She's breathing. But I don't want to move her. Just in case …' he said, his voice trailing off.

She realised after a horrible moment that he meant Michelle might have hurt her back or neck. She swallowed and tried to concentrate.

'I'm coming home,' she said. 'I'll be there as soon as I can.'

'I'll be with her, don't worry,' Charlie said.

Flick put the phone down and pushed herself away from the desk, a million thoughts flying through her mind all at once. A cab would be the fastest way back, so she had to get her purse. She turned towards the door that led to the administration offices, then remembered she'd given her backpack to the concierge for safekeeping. She swivelled back towards the reception desk, suddenly remembering she was at work and that someone had to be in charge of front of house.

'Jacobina, I need you to take over,' she said, barely looking at the other woman. 'My sister's hurt. I have to go to my sister.'

Jacobina gave her a wide-eyed look and reached for her arm.

'Flick, are you okay? What can we do to help?'

'I just have to get home. I have to make sure she's okay,' Flick said, pushing away Jacobina's arm and moving towards the concierge's cubby hole.

She pictured Michelle sprawled in the bathroom, victim of her stupid bath. 'Please let her be all right, please let her be all right.'

Her vision was blurry, and Flick realised with surprise that she was crying. She swiped at the tears impatiently. She didn't have time to cry.

She had to hold it together. Just like she'd been holding it together for the past few months.

'Come on.'

A firm male hand closed around her upper arm, and Flick found herself being propelled towards the front doors of the hotel. Harrison was holding her backpack in his other hand, and he pushed her towards a sleek black car that was parked in front of the hotel. For a moment she didn't understand what was happening, and she resisted the hand that was trying to urge her into the car.

'No, hang on a moment ...' she said, sure that this was wrong.

'Get in the car, Flick. Come on, I'm taking you home,' Harrison said.

And somehow Flick found herself bending and sliding into his car, buckling her seat belt, and bracing herself as he bulldozed his way out into the heavy lunchtime traffic.

And all the while the same refrain was circling in her mind. 'Please let her be all right, please let her be all right.'

Chapter 6

*I*t was the longest drive of Flick's life. Even though her apartment was only a ten-minute taxi ride from the hotel, time seemed to stretch as Harrison expertly navigated his way through the busy traffic. If she hadn't been so worried about Michelle, she might have had time to appreciate the way he shot in and out of lanes, forcing other drivers to give way as he raced her home. His hands were sure and firm on the wheel, and he shifted in and out of gear like a racing pro. But she was only vaguely aware of any of it. When she could see her apartment building in the distance, she slid to the edge of her seat, willing the building to come closer. And then they were out the front, and she was flinging the car door open, shoving her way through the double doors to the foyer, and taking the stairs two at a time.

The door to her apartment was open, and she raced straight through to the bathroom. And gasped with fear as she saw Michelle prone on the floor, blood on the tiles beneath her head, her face pale and blank. She was still wearing her pyjama tank top, she realised, and Charlie had covered her with a couple of towels to keep her warm. He was kneeling next to her, holding her hand, but he stood when he saw Flick.

'She still hasn't woken up,' he reported grimly.

Flick dropped to her knees and reached out to touch Michelle's face. She was half-afraid it would be cold, despite Charlie's reassurances, but her skin was warm and alive to the touch and she cupped her sister's cheek gently.

'Shelly,' was all she said, smoothing the hair back from her sister's forehead. Michelle remained unconscious, and Flick had to fight back terrified tears. Why hadn't she woken up? Her eyes slid to the smear of blood on the tiles beneath Michelle's head. She'd done a first aid course as part of her training at the hotel, and she knew that the longer a person was unconscious, the worse it could be.

Almost as though he could read her mind, Charlie spoke up.

'There's a cut on her scalp, which is why there's so much blood. Scalp wounds bleed pretty bad, even if they're not that deep,' he said.

Flick nodded her understanding. Maybe it was just a scalp wound. But why was Michelle still unconscious, then?

Flick closed her eyes against the tide of self-blame that washed up at her. She shouldn't have given Michelle an ultimatum this morning. She should have kept trying to talk to her, made her spit out what was going on. The sound of footsteps clattering up the stairs drew her attention, and she heard Harrison's deep voice giving directions to the ambulance crew.

'It's number eight, just up here,' he said, and then suddenly there were too many people in too small a space as the ambulance crew crowded in.

Despite wanting to stay with Michelle, Flick stood and eased past the ambulance attendants so they could have access to her sister. Then she hovered in the doorway, Charlie and Harrison standing on either side, watching as they checked Michelle's pupils, took her pulse, and strapped on a spinal collar.

Flick could barely breathe as she watched the ambulance guys talk in medical shorthand to one another. She clenched her hands together, resisting the urge to interrupt and demand to know what was wrong.

A firm hand on her arm drew her attention to Harrison.

'Flick, they're going to have to take your sister to hospital, which means you're going to need your medical insurance details. You're covered, right?' he asked.

Flick stared at him blankly for a moment, trying to make sense of his words. Insurance? Why was he asking about insurance when Michelle still hadn't woken up?

He seemed to understand her lack of comprehension. 'It's not like back home, Flick. They're going to want to know this stuff.'

Suddenly it all made sense, and she nodded.

'Sure, right. Um, Michelle has travel insurance, for two years, I think. The papers are in her case …' she gestured towards the spot where Michelle's case had lived for the past two weeks, but realised it was empty. Then she saw the case, packed and ready to go near the door. Tears filled her eyes as she remembered the argument they'd had that morning.

'It's okay, I'll take care of it,' Harrison said.

In the bathroom, Michelle stirred as one of the paramedics dug his knuckles into her sternum.

Come on, Michelle, wake up for us,' he said.

Flick's knees went weak as Michelle groaned and tried to sit up.

'What's happened? What's going on?' she asked blearily.

'Oh, thank God,' Flick breathed, leaning against the doorway for support.

'You've hurt yourself in the shower, Michelle. We need you to lie still, just in case you've hurt your neck. Can you do that for me?'

Michelle started to cry, and Flick moved forward instinctively, wanting to comfort her.

'Where's Flick? I want my sister,' Michelle said.

Flick moved so that Michelle could see her face over the paramedic's shoulder. 'I'm right here, Shelly. Don't worry, we're going to look after you,' Flick said, swallowing her tears. She needed to be strong for Michelle right now.

Michelle closed her eyes. 'I'm sorry, Flick. I didn't mean any of it …' she said weakly.

'I know, sweetie, it's fine. We'll sort it all out, don't worry,' Flick assured her.

The next few minutes passed in a blur as the paramedics strapped Michelle into a fold-out stretcher and got her ready for transportation to the hospital. Flick stood to one side as they wheeled Michelle past.

'You go in the ambulance with them, and I'll follow,' Harrison said, ushering her towards the door.

'I'll lock up here, don't worry,' Charlie said. He'd hung back in the living room through most of it, and Flick shot him a grateful look.

'Thank you so much, Charlie,' she said. He shrugged and looked embarrassed.

'No problem. You just make sure Michelle's going to be okay,' he said.

Then Harrison was ushering her down the stairs and helping her up into the ambulance. He stood there, a silent, reassuring presence, until the doors closed and they started driving.

Flick sat next to Michelle and held her hand tightly. Michelle's eyelids kept flickering open and closed, as though she was struggling to stay awake. The ambulance attendant leant across and checked her pupils again, then patted her on the arm.

'We need you to try and stay awake for us, Michelle. Can you do that?'

'I'll try,' Michelle mumbled, clearly on the verge of drifting off again.

Flick squeezed her hand tighter to try and get her sister's attention. 'Come on Shelly, don't pike out on us. The man's just going to rub you on the chest again and you know how much that hurts,' she said.

Michelle kept her eyes closed, but screwed up her face in agreement. 'Like when we were little, crow pecks and nipple cripples,' she murmured.

Flick smiled despite everything. Their brother Jack had been a notorious crow-peck inflictor when they were growing up, sneaking up behind his sisters and knocking them sharply on the head with his knuckles. In retaliation, Michelle and Flick would gang up on him and hold him down and give him nipple cripples.

'Exactly like that,' she assured her sister now. 'You even think about going to sleep, and I'm going to authorise this man to give you enough crow pecks to last a life time.'

Michelle smiled faintly, and her eyes flickered open. 'No one could be as bad as Jack,' she said.

Flick kept her sister talking until the ambulance pulled up at the emergency bay at the hospital. The doors hauled open and she was pushed out of the way as Michelle was unloaded from the ambulance. A flock of nurses and doctors surrounded Michelle as they wheeled her into the building, and Flick trailed after them, trying to decipher the shorthand medical talk. When she started to follow Michelle into the treatment room, a brusque nurse put a hand on her chest.

'Sorry, no relatives just yet,' she said, and Flick was forced to stand back as the double doors to the treatment room flapped shut in her face.

With nothing else to do, she paced, glancing in the round windows on the treatment room doors each time she passed by. They were readying Michelle for an x-ray when Harrison joined her.

'What's happening?' he asked.

Flick shrugged, arms crossed tightly over her chest, hands gripping her elbows. 'I don't know. No one's told me anything,' she said.

Harrison nodded his understanding, but when a nurse walked past he stepped forward and cornered her expertly.

'Excuse me. My friend's sister is in there receiving treatment. Would it be possible to get an update on her condition?'

Flick was sure it was his authoritative confidence that sent the nurse straight into the treatment room. She returned a moment later with a smile.

'Okay, they're just doing some film now, but the most likely diagnosis is a fractured skull, or concussion. Someone will be out to let you know as soon as the x-rays are done,' she said.

Flick murmured her thanks and the woman moved away but not before giving Harrison a speculative once over. To his credit, Flick realised that Harrison wasn't even aware of the woman's sexual interest.

Five minutes later, a doctor joined them in the corridor outside.

'You're the sister?' he asked, pulling off a pair of latex gloves.

'Is she going to be all right? Is her skull fractured?' Flick asked, anxiety tightening in her chest.

'No fracture. She does have concussion, however, and I'm concerned by how long she was unconscious. She appears to be lucid, although it's difficult to tell.'

'Michelle's been upset lately, going out a lot. We had a fight about it this morning,' she explained. She could feel Harrison watching her, but she didn't take her eyes from the doctor.

'We're going to keep her in overnight, keep an eye on her. Hourly observations just to make sure there's nothing we've missed. But she should be right to go home after that, all things being equal,' the doctor said.

Flick thanked him for his time, her shoulders sagging as she absorbed what he'd said: Michelle was going to be okay.

'Here,' Harrison said. He placed a hand on the small of her back and pushed her gently towards a nearby bench.

Flick sat down gratefully, a wave of exhaustion washing over her. With the tiredness came awareness that Michelle might not have been so lucky, and she couldn't hold onto her tears any more. The habit of protecting herself from Harrison was so strong that she tried to hide her face from him, dashing the tears away with her hands.

'Flick,' he said, sitting beside her. And then he pulled her into his arms and soothed a hand down her back.

For a heartbeat she resisted him, remembering all the cruel, hard things he'd said and done over the past few weeks. Then she gave in to the need to be comforted, pressing her face into his shoulder and clinging to a handful of his shirt. After a few minutes, the tears passed and she slowly pulled away from him. A big wet patch decorated one shoulder of his shirt, and she brushed at it ineffectually.

'I've made you all soggy,' she said stupidly.

'It doesn't matter.'

She glanced away from the intent look in his eyes, confused. He'd been so nice, so supportive and thoughtful.

'I'm not really sure why you're here,' she blurted suddenly.

He looked uncomfortable for a second then shrugged a shoulder.

'Maybe I'm not, either. But when I realised something was wrong, I didn't want you to have to deal with it on your own.'

Flick stared at him, even more confused now. He reached into his pocket and pulled out a handkerchief, and leaned forward to dry the tears from her cheeks. His touch was gentle and tender, and Flick lifted up a hand to still him, pushing his hand away.

'Don't, Harrison,' she said. When he turned on the charm, it was almost possible to forget the way he'd behaved for the past few months. But she couldn't forget that he was already spoken for. The thought of his wife stiffened her spine. 'You've been really terrific today, but what happened between you and me on that first night was a mistake. I don't care what you think of me, I don't go out with married men,' she said clearly.

He actually flinched, his head jerking back as though she'd slapped him. Then his mouth crooked into a quick, incredulous grin.

'I'm not married, Felicity,' he said.

She frowned at him. What game was he trying to play now?

'Yes you are. I remember—Marc was best man at your wedding,' she said.

'Sure, I was married. I guess if we're being technical, I still am. But I separated from my wife more than six months ago, and the divorce will be final as soon as my lawyers can arrange it.'

She was surprised at the sense of relief she felt. But, after all, it didn't really mean anything. At the end of the day, he still thought she was some sort of home-wrecker. And she refused to forget how horrible he'd been for the past two months.

'I can't believe you thought I was still married,' he said, shaking his head in disbelief.

'Ms Scully? You can go in to your sister now.'

Flick snapped around to face the nurse who was standing in the doorway to Michelle's room.

'Thank you,' she said, standing. Stiff, she turned to Harrison. 'Thanks for everything. Michelle and I really appreciate it, but we'll be okay from here on in,' she said formally.

He looked nonplussed at being dismissed, but she didn't have time for him right now.

'Flick, I—' he said, but she just shook her head at him and followed the nurse into Michelle's room.

Michelle had a bandage wrapped around her hairline, and a blood pressure cuff was secured to her arm. Her eyes were closed, but when Flick approached the bed they flickered open.

'Hi,' Flick said gently.

'Hi. I've got stitches,' Michelle said.

'Yeah, I know. I've got grey hair,' Flick said.

Michelle smiled, but the light quickly faded from her eyes. 'I'm sorry about what I said. It was stupid. I'm sorry about all of it.'

'It's okay, Shelly. We can talk about it later. You just concentrate on getting better,' Flick said.

Michelle smiled at her, and Flick sat down beside the bed and took her sister's hand. Something made her glance towards the doorway, and she saw Harrison's face framed in the round window. When he saw her watching, he nodded his head once in acknowledgement then walked away. Flick bit her lip, aware that she didn't want him to go.

Which was stupid, because up until a few hours ago she'd hated the sight of the man. Confused, she turned back to Michelle. Harrison Lambert could look after himself.

Harrison sat in his car for a long time after he'd left the hospital. He kept seeing the colour drain from Flick's face as she learnt that her sister had been injured. The look in her eyes had made his stomach clench with dread. He'd wanted to put his arms around her and assure her that everything would be all right, that he'd protect her and keep her from harm.

Pretty big turnaround from wanting her gone from his hotel, and keeping tabs on her every move so he could do just that. Pretty big turnaround.

Which was why he was sitting in his car, trying to make sense of his warring emotions. Bottom line: he had never stopped finding her attractive. And now he was beginning to think that his initial snap judgement at finding out her real identity had been way off.

For starters, it had stunned him to learn that she'd thought he was married. It explained an enormous amount of her antagonism towards him. And also showed what she thought of infidelity.

He realised that in all the time that he'd worked with Flick, he'd never seen her act without integrity. She was a hard worker, and she trusted her staff. That trust was well rewarded—she ran one of the best front of house operations he'd ever seen in the Lassiter's chain. She was liked and respected by her colleagues. Leo thought the world of her. In hundreds of ways, every time he saw her she proved to him that she was far more than a shallow girl who'd broken up her sister's wedding on a whim. He was beginning to realise that maybe he'd made a big misstep where Felicity Scully was concerned. And that that misstep may have cost him the chance to get to know the real Flick. And the more he realised how big his mistake was, the more he realised that he was the one who was going to miss out in this equation.

Acting on autopilot, he drove back to the hotel and checked in with Jacobina and Leo to fill them in on what was happening with Flick and her sister. As he'd suspected, they were sympathetic and supportive. He decided to ignore the speculative glances Leo kept throwing his way. Rushing Flick from the building like that probably hadn't been the most discrete move he could have pulled, but he didn't regret it for a minute. She'd needed help, and he'd wanted to be the one to offer it.

Which was why he found himself shutting down his computer at six o'clock on the dot, and striding out of the building. A quick stop at his favourite Italian restaurant, and he was on his way back to the hospital.

His step slowed as he approached Michelle's room. Impulse and instinct had brought him here, but he honestly didn't know if he would be welcome. He probably didn't deserve to be welcome, given the way he'd been behaving the past few months. But he had to go in. He needed to see Flick, needed to make sure she was holding up. At the very least, he could offer her a meal. At best, she might let him share it with her.

She was sitting in a chair beside Michelle's bed. Michelle was asleep, and Flick's head was resting back on the chair, her eyes closed. He hesitated, not wanting to disturb either of them. Then she opened her eyes. They were filled with wariness as she registered his presence.

'Hi,' he said softly. He lifted the bag containing the takeaway 'I thought you might be hungry.'

She stared at him for a moment, then pushed herself up out of the chair and signalled for him to move ahead of her out into the corridor. Only when the door was closed on her sister did she turn to him.

Her brow was wrinkled into a frown, and confusion was clear on her face as she regarded him.

'It's just dinner, Flick,' he said. But they both knew it was a lot more than that.

'Why are you here?' she asked simply.

Harrison sighed deeply and realised that at the very least he owed her an explanation. He gestured towards the bench seat running along the wall, and they both sat down.

For a moment Harrison studied his hands, trying to find the words.

'When we first met, I was instantly attracted to you,' he began. 'Not just because you're beautiful—which you are, of course—but because I liked you. That first night … I couldn't get you out of my head. Then I found out who you were.'

'And you decided to judge me before you even had a conversation with me about it,' Flick shot back at him.

Harrison ran his hand through his hair, trying to find a way to make her understand. He'd been so bitter about everything with Amanda. And then he'd met Flick, and found her so attractive and quickly discovered she was the woman who had broken his brother's heart.

'My wife and I were married for nearly five years,' he said slowly. 'I thought we were pretty happy. I travelled a lot, for work, you know, but when we were together, things were good. But she'd been sleeping around behind my back for years. And I only found out when I caught her leaving one of our hotels with her lover.'

His face hardened as he remembered that day again: the look on her face, the humiliation and anger he'd felt.

'What does any of this have to do with me?' Flick prompted when he was silent for too long.

He looked at her, and realisation dawned. He sat back and pressed his fingers to the bridge of his nose.

'Jesus,' he said, shaking his head at his own stupidity.

What had any of this to do with Flick? Nothing. Absolutely nothing. But he had tarred her with the same brush as his soon-to-be-ex-wife, had punished her as though she was Amanda, said things to her that were meant for Amanda.

He'd been so bent out of shape over what had happened with his wife that he'd been ready and raring to take a shot at anyone. And poor Flick had walked straight between his crosshair.

'Flick, I owe you an apology,' he said, looking her square in the eye. 'I have been unfair to you. Very unfair. I used to think I was a man who judged people on their merits, someone who made his own decisions. But I threw all that out the window when I realised who you were. Because of what happened with my wife, because I've been so angry and messed up about what happened, I took it out on you. I chose to believe what I'd been told about you over what I saw with my own eyes.'

He stood, handing over the bag of Italian food.

'I came here tonight because I wanted to help you. But I realise now I don't have the right. I've been terrible, I know that. I'm sorry, for what it's worth.'

He looked down at her, taking in the exotic slope of her cheekbone, the clear mahogany of her eyes. She'd never flinched, never backed down in all the time he'd been persecuting her. She was tough, and brave. And probably a lot of other great things he'd never get the chance to find out.

Nodding once, he turned on his heel and started walking.

Flick watched him walk away, her fingers clenched tightly around the plastic handle of the carrier bag. She didn't know what to do with what he'd just said to her. But she also knew that she didn't want him to leave.

'Harrison, wait,' she said.

He turned back to face her, and she could

see the tension in his whole body as he waited for her to speak again. She smiled and held up the bag with the takeaway.

'You don't expect me to eat all this on my own, do you?'

The smile that swept across his face chased away all her doubts. He had made a mistake, judging her the way he did. But he'd had his reasons, and she of all people knew that people were so much more than the choices they made, be they good or bad.

And she knew that it was possible to learn from them and move on.

He sat back down beside her on the bench, reaching for the topmost foil container.

'I got a double serve of the cannelloni, it's the best thing you've ever tasted,' he said.

Half an hour later, her belly was full and she was feeling more relaxed than she had been in months. Of course, it helped that the main cause of stress in her life had apologised, and was sitting next to her, trying to force the last chocolate mousse-filled cannoli down despite the fact that she was full to bursting. But it was more than that. This felt right. It had that first night, too. There was something about Harrison that drew her, and she knew now that he felt the same. It was in every look they shared, every accidental brush of their hands. It was in the heat of his body as he sat next to her on the hard wooden bench. This was special. This was something big.

When they'd finished eating they went back in to join Michelle just as the nurse entered to wake her for her hourly observation. So far there had been no obvious side effects from her concussion, and Flick brushed a strand of hair away from her sister's forehead and prayed that it would stay that way.

'Why can I smell garlic?' Michelle asked when the nurse left.

Flick shot Harrison a guilty look. They hadn't thought to save any for Michelle.

'Harrison brought some Italian in,' she explained. 'We can get more if you're hungry?'

But Michelle just screwed up her nose. 'No food. Head's aching too much.'

Flick frowned. 'They've given you something for that, though, right? I'll tell the nurse you need more.'

'I'll find her,' Harrison offered even as she rose from her chair beside Michelle's bed.

She watched him exit, allowing herself to admire the broadness of his shoulders. It was nice to have someone looking out for her, she admitted to herself. It felt like a long time since she'd had someone fighting in her corner.

Harrison returned with a nurse, and Michelle dutifully swallowed a couple of painkillers. Harrison sat on the other side of the bed, and between the two of them they kept Michelle amused for a couple of hours, telling horror stories from the hotel.

After a while, Michelle's eyelids started to droop, and Harrison and Flick fell silent. Even though Michelle would still be woken for hourly observations through the rest of the night, it was good for her to sleep—as long as it was genuine rest and not symptomatic of anything more insidious.

Harrison went for a walk and brought back coffees, and for a while they sat quietly side by side, whispering over the puzzle page of a magazine they'd found in the waiting area. When the nurse arrived for her next set of observations, Michelle frowned at them clearly puzzled to see they were still there.

'Go home,' Michelle ordered. 'You look exhausted, Flick. I'll be fine.'

Flick shook her head. There was no way she was leaving her concussed baby sister all alone in a New York hospital.

'Sorry, no can do. Besides, one night of bad sleep won't kill me,' she said airily.

'But what about tomorrow, when I get to come home? You'll be even more tired, and I'll need you to be on the ball for me then,' Michelle pointed out.

Harrison caught Flick's eye. 'I think she's right. You look like you've run a marathon.'

Flick thought back over the events of the day: getting up early to confront Michelle about her behaviour, their fight, then the crisis at work, then rushing home to Michelle. It had been an exhausting day, and she was feeling very fragile.

'Go on, go home,' Michelle urged, sensing she was weakening.

'As long as you promise to get them to call me if anything changes. And I mean anything,' Flick said.

After heartfelt vows from Michelle that she would be phoned the instant anything altered and a big hug and kiss goodbye, Flick found herself exiting the hospital, Harrison's hand warm on the small of her back.

This time she took note of the sleek black car he led her to—a Porsche convertible, with a dark burgundy leather interior. As she sank into the bucket seat and pulled her seatbelt on, she slid a nervous glance across at him. She couldn't quite believe that the cold war they'd been waging for the past few months was over. Harrison caught her glance.

'You warm enough? Want the heater on?' he asked solicitously.

She marvelled that she was once again the recipient of his warm, intent regard. That his eyes could be so gentle and attractive, when previously they had been ice-cold and hard.

They drove in silence, Flick watching the smooth, practiced way his hands moved on the steering wheel. Before she knew it, they were pulling up out the front of her apartment building.

Harrison came around to open her car door, and she realised he intended to escort her all the way up to the fourth floor. They climbed the stairs slowly, and Flick admitted to herself that she didn't want this night to be over just yet. As they approached her front door, she took her courage in both hands and turned to face him.

'Would you like to come in for a little while?' she asked in a rush.

He just smiled, and took the keys from her hands. A quick glance around the apartment revealed that Charlie had not only locked up, but he'd also cleaned up the mess in the bathroom. He'd even left a note on the fridge to say that he had returned the spare key to Mr Mustaffa, and that he'd left some cookies he'd baked that afternoon on the bench.

Harrison raised his eyebrows as he read the note. 'What a guy,' he said a little flatly, and Flick grinned as she picked up on the jealousy in his voice.

'Relax. He's got the hots for Michelle,' she said.

Harrison smiled and reached for the container full of cookies. 'In that case, I'm starving,' he said.

Flick made coffee, and by mutual consent they crawled out the window and sat opposite each other on the fire escape to enjoy their impromptu feast. With cushions from the couch to soften the hard metal of the landing, and a candle stuck to the windowsill with a gob of wax, it felt like their own private little slice of paradise.

Flick marvelled over how many cookies Harrison packed away, and he spread his palms wide and shrugged.

'Can you blame me? Dinner was hours ago. I'm a growing boy.'

Flick raised an eyebrow. 'You'll be growing in the wrong direction if you keep that up.'

Harrison patted his perfectly flat belly. 'Everyone says once you hit thirty it's all downhill.'

'I think you'll survive,' she said, eyeing him appreciatively.

'Careful, Ms Scully. A man could misconstrue a look like that.'

Flick blushed, feeling as though she had revealed a little too much.

'So, do you miss Australia?' he asked, deftly changing the subject.

She smiled at him gratefully. 'Only a lot.

Everything's so different over here. Exciting and all that, but there's something about Australia … I was running through Central Park last month, and there were a couple of gum trees alongside the path. The smell! It seriously stopped me in my tracks it smelt so much like home. And there's something about the colour of the sky back home. It just seems higher and bluer.'

She realised Harrison was watching her with a small smile on his lips.

'I suppose that makes me sound pathetically homesick, but I'm not.'

'I know. There's no place like home, but it's okay to be somewhere else, too,' he said.

She nudged him with her toe. 'How come you're so good at saying exactly what I'm thinking?' she asked.

They smiled at each other again. A chill breeze whipped around the corner of the building, and Flick shivered. Harrison looked concerned.

'Time to go in?' he asked, reaching for their coffee cups. But Flick was enjoying it all too much.

'No way. Time for you to make us another coffee and bring me out a blanket,' she said.

He didn't need to be asked twice, and she knew he was savouring this as much as she was. It was as though they'd saved up all this talk and getting-to-know-you stuff for months, and it had just been sitting there, waiting to come out while they took shots at each other.

And so they talked, and laughed, and confessed, and shared until the candle was flickering in a pool of wax. They spoke about their childhoods, and their experiences at school, and Harrison told her about his marriage, and she told him about Marc and her sister and the mess she'd made of it all. They talked about Michelle and Connor, and how best to manage things in the future. They argued about movies and books, and agreed on politics, and discovered that they both secretly loved bad American reality TV shows.

But at last the wavering candle could no longer be ignored. As it flickered in its death throes, Harrison reluctantly looked at his watch.

'Three o'clock. I should go,' he said.

But they both remained where they were. Flick could feel her heart pounding against her ribs as she waited for him to say or do something else. Well, more specifically, for him to kiss her. And then she realised that maybe she should take the initiative, being a modern woman and all, and she crawled across the small space and took his face between her hands. For a long moment she gazed into his eyes, dark navy and mysterious in the moonlight, and then she lowered her head and kissed him. It wasn't like that first kiss. This kiss was gentle and slow, a promise of more kisses to come. And then Harrison hauled her closer, and she was lying in his arms, and he was kissing her as though there was no tomorrow.

After a time, he lifted his head and kissed her on each closed eyelids and smoothed a hand over her hair.

'Now I really have to go,' he said, his voice a low rumble that vibrated through her body.

Flick stirred and pushed herself away from him. She was falling in love with this man, she realised. In fact, she'd been half in love with him since she'd met him, despite everything. Part of her wanted to ask him to stay the night, but they'd just had an incredible evening of intimacy and revelation. It felt right to leave it like this. Tomorrow was a new day, and they could put the misunderstandings of the past behind them and move on.

Slowly they climbed back into the apartment, Flick only then realising how stiff and sore her muscles were from being in one position too long. She yawned hugely, and laughed when she saw Harrison doing the same.

'Why are yawns so contagious?' he asked.

She had no answer for him, and they found themselves at the front door, both of them reluctant to say the final goodbye.

'Get some sleep. And don't bother about coming in tomorrow. I'll square things with Leo. I have a little influence in that area,' he said, pretending to buff his fingernails on his jacket.

'I'd heard that. Just make sure you use your powers for good instead of evil,' Flick teased back.

He grew serious for a moment, and pulled her close for one last kiss.

'Forever and always. I've learnt my lesson, Flick Scully. I nearly missed out on the best thing to come my way in a long time.'

He ran a finger down her cheek then brushed his thumb across her mouth.

'Sleep tight.'

Flick closed the door on him with a sigh, leaning her forehead against the wood for a few seconds, waiting for the sound of him descending the stairs.

'Make sure you set both the locks,' he called out, his voice muffled by the door.

She smiled to herself and clicked both the bolts home. She heard his step on the stairs, and turned and walked through to her bedroom.

The sight of her bed brought home exactly how tired she was, and she threw herself on it fully clothed. It had been a terrible day, but a beautiful night, and she fell asleep with a smile on her lips.

Chapter 7

*H*arrison smiled to the night staff as he crossed the foyer to the lift. It was after four in the morning, and his eyes felt gritty with tiredness, but his mind was full of Flick.

She was the most amazing woman he'd ever met, and he wanted to know everything about her, as quickly as possible. With Amanda, he'd fallen into a commitment, following the well-travelled road from attraction to comfortable habit and finally to marriage. It had seemed like the right thing. Of course he had loved her, he would never deny that, but he'd never felt this kind of yearning for her. Even though he'd just left Flick, he wanted to be with her again. He couldn't get enough of her: she was like a fever in his blood.

She was different from anyone else he'd ever dated. She was young, but she was grounded and earthy and wise, and she knew what she wanted from life, and what she was prepared to do to get it. Hard won self-knowledge, he knew, after talking to her all night. And she was funny, and self-aware, and she called a spade a spade—a characteristic that was sadly lacking in many of the women he encountered on the social circuit. She was also fiercely loyal to her family, even more so after what had happened between her and Marc. As uncomfortable as it had been listening to her talk about that disastrous time, it had been important. He felt that he understood now. She had made a mistake, but who was he to judge? He had a failed marriage and some pretty bad judgement calls on his own record. Neither of them came to this relationship without baggage.

Harrison caught his reflection in the mirrored panel inside the lift. He was grinning like a loon, but he couldn't stop. Relationship. He had absolutely no doubt that he and Felicity Scully had a relationship to explore now. He wanted to spend more time with her, to make her laugh, and to laugh at her own unique, dry take on the world. He wanted to kiss her and more, and if he hadn't been so determined to do it right this time, he would still be with her, sharing her bed, holding her close.

But it had been a great night, even if he was going home alone. A great night and the first of many more. If someone had dared to tell him that he would be feeling this way about someone so soon after what had happened with Amanda, he would have laughed in their face. But it had been out of his hands the moment he looked into her eyes as she stood dripping wet in her maid's uniform all those months ago. From that moment on, he'd been fighting a losing battle against his desire to be with her. And now the fight was over—she was his.

He knew there were a few potential complications on the horizon. His divorce, for one; and his family, for another. But all of it paled into insignificance when he thought about Flick. He wanted to be with her. It was that simple.

A huge yawn snuck up on him, and Harrison closed his eyes and gave into it as the lift pinged to a halt at the penthouse. Rubbing a hand across his eyes, he swiped his pass card in the door lock and entered the suite. The curtains were still open, and the lights of Manhattan twinkled below him as he crossed the darkened living room to press the button to close the drapes.

'About time. Let me guess, you've been out clubbing with some hot chicky babe but she let you down at the last moment.'

Harrison whirled on his heel, adrenalin surging through him before he recognised his brother's voice.

'Jesus, Marc, you scared the living daylights out of me,' he said.

The table-lamp clicked on, and he saw that Marc was stretched out full-length on the sofa, his shoes discarded on the floor alongside a travel magazine. Laughing, Marc tossed a cushion at him.

'Surprise! Guess I'm lucky you came home at all. Do you have any idea how long I've been hanging around waiting for you?'

Marc was grinning up at him, but all Harrison could think about was Flick, and what Marc's presence might mean for their burgeoning relationship. The smile on Marc's face faded a little as the silence stretched between them.

'Wow, knock me over with the warm welcome, Harry,' he said. There was a dark look in his eye, and Harrison shook off the feelings of guilt and discomfort. Marc and Flick were over a long time ago; there was nothing for him to worry about.

'Of course I'm glad to see you. I just need to go change my underwear now, thanks,' Harrison said, moving forward to embrace his brother.

Marc stood, returning the hug fiercely and clapping a hand on Harrison's back.

'For a moment there I thought you were about to give me a Mum-style pep-talk,' he said, settling back on the sofa again.

Harrison toed off his shoes and sank into an armchair. As he relaxed back into the soft leather upholstery, he registered the large bottle of whisky sitting on the floor near Marc.

'Why would it matter if I'd been talking to Chloe?' Harrison asked. He'd given up calling her mum when he joined the management team at Lassiter's.

Marc shrugged, his eyes sliding away. Harrison frowned. He hadn't seen Marc for a while. In fact, it had probably been more than a year. At Christmas, Marc had been travelling somewhere, a hangover from the round-the-world trip he'd taken to get Flick out of his system.

Harrison shifted in his seat, uneasy at the thought of Flick again. Stupid to think that this was anything to do with her but he still felt on edge.

'She's been on my case, that's all. Wants me to make a decision about where I want to be based, what I want to do,' Marc said, reaching for the whisky bottle.

He raised an eyebrow at Harrison, and he nodded his agreement to a drink. 'Is that so unreasonable, wanting you to pick a posting? You have to settle into something sometime,' Harrison suggested, accepting a generous tumbler of whisky from his brother. 'Can't expect to manage one of the chains without sticking with a hotel for a while and learning the ropes.'

The dark look shadowed Marc's eyes again, and he took a big swig from his whisky.

'Maybe I'm not interested in any of that. Maybe I don't want to be a part of the Lambert hotel empire.'

Harrison studied his younger brother, noticing for the first time the new lines around his eyes and mouth, the unruly length of his hair, the way his hands never seemed to stay still. Marc stank of unhappiness and discontent, he realised. Having suffered from it himself recently, he knew the symptoms intimately.

'Want to throw it all in and become an artist or something, mate?' he asked lightly, watching Marc carefully.

Marc leant forward, elbows braced on his knees, his face urgent.

'Have you ever thought that maybe you found the one thing in your life that could make you happy, but you let it slip through your fingers? And now you have to spend the rest of your life knowing you stuffed up?'

Harrison felt a slow, dread-filled weight settle in his stomach. This was about Flick; he knew it, absolutely. Still, he hoped.

'I take it you think you've stuffed up somewhere along the line?' he fished.

Marc ran a hand through his hair and took another swig from his whisky.

'I had her, you know. I had her, but I stuffed it up. I should have just broken up with Steph before the wedding. If I'd had enough guts to do it then, everything would have been different. Then we could have waited until the heat died down, and she wouldn't have felt so bad. She said that nothing could be built on the foundation we had. Maybe she was right. But she was the one thing in my life that was good, you know?' Marc said, his voice tight and intense.

Misery and urgency radiated off him, and Harrison pushed his whisky away, a bitter taste in his mouth. The irony of the situation didn't escape him, of course. Here he was, falling hard for Felicity Scully—the same woman that his brother was now telling him he'd never gotten over. A warped echo of what had happened back home in Australia. If he let things go that way.

'Is that why you're here?' he asked slowly.

Marc lifted suspiciously bright eyes to him then knuckled away the moisture impatiently.

'I can't get her out of my head. No matter where I go, or what I do, she's there. All the 'what ifs' are driving me crazy.'

Harrison closed his eyes for a moment, remembering the look in Flick's eyes when she'd kissed him tonight. Was he really man enough to back away from that for his brother's sake?

'I was thinking that maybe it's been long enough now. Maybe we could start fresh,' Marc said. His expression was pleading, begging for Harrison to agree with him.

Again he thought of Flick, the curve of her cheekbone, the slim strength of her body.

'Sure. You don't want to die not knowing, do you?' Harrison heard himself say in a strange, flat tone.

So, there it was. Apparently he was going to do the right thing. Very damned noble of him.

'That's what I figured. So I'm here, and I'm going to lay it all on the line and see what happens. She loved me once. That doesn't just disappear, does it?' Marc asked.

'Mate, I'm going to turn in,' Harrison said abruptly, unable to have this conversation. It was one thing to step back, and another thing to promote a match between Flick and Marc. 'Help yourself to one of the other rooms.'

Marc stared up at him for a moment, then nodded. 'Sure, thanks. And thanks for listening.'

'No problem,' Harrison assured him.

Then he walked away, wondering all the while why doing the right thing felt so wrong, and knowing that it was only going to get worse over the coming weeks.

Flick woke at her usual time, rang the hospital to check that Michelle was well, then rolled over and got an extra couple of hours sleep. She woke feeling light-hearted and filled with anticipation. She wasn't quite sure what she was anticipating, but it had to do with Harrison, and she knew it was good.

She sang in the shower, a stupid made up song about love, and she padded into the kitchen to make coffee and toast with a big smile on her face. She was just spreading jam on her third piece of toast when the security intercom sounded.

She pressed the call button, licking butter off her fingers. 'Who is it?'

Traffic noise crackled at her, but she caught the most important word—Lambert. She grinned, unable to help herself, and pressed the call button again.

'Come on up!' she said.

Quickly she crossed to the bathroom to check she looked reasonably presentable, tightening the sash on her pink silk dressing gown as she went. Her hair was still damp, but there was nothing she could do about that, and she had to be satisfied with running a quick dash of lipstick across her lips. She spun away from the mirror at the knock on the door, and raced across to answer it. Pulling the door open, she felt a surge of joy that Harrison had been unable to stay away. It must mean that he felt the same way as her. He was older, more experienced than her, but surely what she'd felt last night couldn't be one-sided. Surely he was feeling as drawn to her as she was to him.

But her pleasure soured abruptly as she registered which Lambert was standing on her doorstep—not Harrison, but Marc. A scruffier, more tired version of Marc, but Marc nonetheless.

'What are you doing here?' she asked, stunned.

He offered a smile. 'Surprise! Can I come in?'

Flick stared at him, grappling with a cascade of emotions, none of them positive.

'Marc, I—'

'I just want to talk,' he said. He gestured for her to precede him into the apartment, and Flick was so stunned she did. Aware of how underdressed she was, she tugged protectively at the neckline of her dressing gown.

'I need to go change,' she said abruptly.

Marc shrugged, offering another smile. 'Not on my account. You look beautiful, Flick.'

Deeply uncomfortable, Flick ducked her head and walked through to her bedroom, a thousand questions clamouring at her. Why was he here? Did Harrison know he was in town? If so, why hadn't he warned her?

Flick pulled on a pair of tracksuit pants and a T-shirt, aware that her stomach was churning with anxiety. Why was he here?

Finally she was ready. She found him in the kitchen, pouring two cups of coffee. He slid one towards her.

'This place is great,' he said enthusiastically. 'A real New York pad.'

Flick left the coffee cup where it was on the bench.

'Marc, why are you here?' she asked.

He took a mouthful of coffee before he responded. 'It's been a long time, Flick. Nearly three years.'

She just held his eye, waiting for him to get to the point.

'Okay, I'm just going to lay it on the line here. I know it's been a while, but I was hoping … well, I was wondering, really, if you would like to go out for dinner tonight,' Marc asked.

His blue eyes were hopeful as they scanned her face.

'Dinner? You want to go out for dinner?' she repeated stupidly, not quite getting what he was asking.

'Yeah. The thing is, Flick, that I just can't seem to get over you,' he said. He half-smiled, some of the old roguish charm twinkling in his eyes. 'So here I am, throwing myself at your feet and wondering if we couldn't try to get it right this time around.'

Flick stared at him, her throat closing with dismay. Marc wanted to pick up where they'd left off. She couldn't quite believe it. Just last night, she'd made a connection with Harrison that felt more powerful and more profound than anything she'd ever experienced with another man. And now Marc was on her doorstep, his heart in his hands, asking her to try again.

Words of rejection were quick on her tongue, but she closed her lips over them, mostly because they all involved Harrison. She couldn't tell Marc she was involved with his brother—could she? Not until she spoke to him, found out what he felt, how he wanted to handle this.

'Aren't you just a little bit pleased to see me?' Marc asked.

Flick didn't know what to say to him. The last thing she wanted was to take up with Marc Lambert again. Even if she hadn't met Harrison, even if she wasn't in love with him, she would feel the same way. What had happened between her and Marc was a mistake. An ugly, messy mistake that had broken her sister's heart. She could never look at Marc without remembering that day, and the look on her sister's face as Marc stumbled over his vows at the altar, then turned to stare at her. Steph's face had been filled with a dawning anger and hurt as she turned to face Flick, too, and then the only thing Flick could think to do was run, just get out of there as quickly as possible.

'Marc, I'm sorry, but I don't think this was such a great idea,' she began.

Marc reached out for her, and she instinctively stepped backwards to avoid his touch.

'I can't come to dinner with you, and I can't give us another chance,' she said very clearly. 'What happened between us is over. We can't go back.'

'Just think about it, Flick, that's all I ask,' Marc said.

'I don't want to. I don't need to. I don't love you, Marc. I have a whole new life now. I'm happy. Things have changed.'

'Not for me. I can't forget you. Don't you understand that?' he said. There was the flicker of anger in his face now, as though he hated admitting this stuff to her, but couldn't help himself.

'I'm sorry. But it doesn't change the way I feel,' she said.

She crossed to the door and held it open. Marc stared across at her, his expression dark and brooding.

'You loved me once. I know you did,' he said.

'It was more than three years ago, Marc. And loving you nearly cost me my family. And my self-respect.'

A muscle tensed in his jaw, and then he broke eye contact with her and scanned the room as though it might provide the answer he was looking for.

'Okay, I'll go,' he said after a tense silence. He crossed to the door, and Flick just managed to stop herself from pulling away from him again when he reached out a hand and brushed a finger along her cheek.

'But I'm not giving up, Flick. I've spent too long regretting ever letting you go to make the same mistake twice. You'll be hearing from me,' he said.

It was only after she'd shut the door that Flick realised she'd been holding her breath. Her first instinct was to talk to Harrison, to see if he knew Marc was in town, and she pulled her mobile phone from her backpack and dialled his number. The phone cut across to his message service, and she found herself listening to the beep of the recording with no idea what to say.

'Um, hi, it's Flick. I guess I'll … speak to you later,' she said.

Her toast was sitting cold and uneaten on the kitchen bench, but she didn't want it now; her stomach was tight with anxiety, and she dumped the lot in the bin.

She didn't know what to do. And she desperately needed to talk to Harrison. They hadn't talked about how Marc might deal with their hooking up last night. It hadn't been an issue, then. Of course, they'd both known that there might be problems to overcome, but they hadn't seemed insurmountable. Now Marc had shown up out of the blue and all the problems she'd avoided thinking about were front and centre.

Flick made a frustrated noise in the back of her throat and threw her head back. Why did this always happen to her? Couldn't she just fall in love with a guy who was free to love her so they could live happily ever after? Was that asking too much?

She did a couple of laps of the living room then shook her head at her own dramatics. She was overreacting. She had to be. After last night, there was no doubting the way Harrison felt about her. That was the important thing.

The wall clock caught her eye and she released a pent-up sigh. It was time to go see Michelle. Grabbing her keys, she slung her backpack over her shoulder and headed out the door.

By the time she was walking in the automatic doors of the hospital, she'd calmed down significantly. Marc showing up was a problem, yes, but not an insurmountable one. It just meant she and Harrison had to deal with the situation a little sooner than expected, that was all.

Michelle was sitting up in bed polishing off a bowl of cereal. She looked pleased when she saw Flick, but almost immediately blushed a deep red and broke eye contact. Feeling a little ashamed, Flick guessed.

'How are you doing?' she asked as she dumped her backpack by the bed.

'Good. Headache all gone. The doctor said if my obs are normal at the morning round I can go home,' she said.

'That's great. I brought you some clothes, and we can get a taxi,' Flick said.

'Cool.'

Now that the immediacy of the tension and anxiety of yesterday had dissipated there was an awkwardness between them. Flick tried hard to dispel it.

'I'm not angry with you, if that's what you're worried about,' she said lightly.

Michelle fiddled with the sheet on her bed. 'I know. I just feel so stupid. I can't believe that Charlie found me.'

Flick smiled faintly—so that was what this was all about. Michelle was having an attack of post-traumatic modesty.

'You had your PJ top on still, Shelly, and your knickers, if that's what you're worried about. Apparently you were trying to have a shower in your clothes,' she said dryly.

Michelle looked hugely relieved. 'Thank God! I thought he'd found me naked on the bathroom floor. I can hardly remember anything from yesterday.'

Flick gave her a measuring look. 'I can remember enough for both of us, don't worry.'

Michelle looked guilty and broke eye contact again. 'I'm sorry. I didn't mean for any of that to happen. And I didn't mean any of that stuff I said to you. I was just … angry, I guess.'

'I know, Shelly. But drinking and staying out late is no way to deal with your feelings. Would it really be so horrible to talk to me about it?' Flick asked.

Michelle shrugged a shoulder, plucking at the sheet again. 'There really isn't anything to talk about. I was just partying a bit hard, that's all.'

Flick made a rude noise. 'Michelle, you were partying like the world was about to end. And we both know it wasn't about having fun. You were upset about Connor.'

It wasn't a guess, it was a statement of fact. Michelle plucked at the sheet, eyes steadfastly downcast.

'It doesn't matter. It won't happen again,' she said.

'Shelly, please. Talk to me. Tell me what's going on in that head of yours,' Flick pleaded.

But Michelle wouldn't look up. 'I'm okay. It's okay. I just had to get him out of my system, that's all.'

Flick felt like grabbing Michelle and shaking the truth out of her, but that wasn't going to help anything. And maybe hospital wasn't the best place for this discussion—and probably she wasn't in the best place herself right now, given Marc's sudden reappearance in her life.

The thought of Marc made her check her mobile, but there was no message from Harrison. She eyed the blank phone display disconsolately.

Why hadn't he called?

A million and one ideas presented themselves to her, many of them paranoid and far-fetched. It was all so new, that was the problem. If Marc had turned up next week, or, better, next month, she and Harrison would have had a chance to consolidate their relationship. As it was, he'd turned up at exactly the wrong time.

Michelle was discharged with the morning round, and they took a taxi back to the apartment. It wasn't until Flick had paid the driver and was heading for the front doors to the building that she registered Harrison's car parked out the front. She met his eyes in the rear view mirror, and he unfolded himself from the car and stood to meet her. Michelle looked from one to the other, clearly sensing that something was up.

'I'll go upstairs,' she said, and Flick threw her the front door keys.

He looked tired, Flick thought as she approached him. Tired and wary.

'I take it you know about Marc,' she said. It was in every line of his body, he might as well have yelled it up the street.

'I'm sorry I didn't get a chance to warn you. I didn't realise he was planning on coming over here first thing until he told me afterwards,' Harrison said. He sounded stiff and uncomfortable, and Flick realised that something bad was about to happen.

'Is that why you didn't return my call?' she asked.

He just stared at her, his face tense. She waited, holding eye contact.

'He still loves you, Flick,' he said at last. 'He thinks you're the love of his life.'

'He's wrong. What we had is over,' she said.

For a second a fierce, pleased light shone in Harrison's eyes.

'Last night was really special for me, Harrison,' she said softly. The words 'I love you' trembled on her lips, but before she could say them Harrison spoke again.

'He loves you, Flick,' he repeated.

She shook her head. 'I don't love him. You know that,' she said. 'After last night, you know that.'

She reached out a hand towards him, wanting to emphasise her point. Harrison caught her hand before it touched his arm.

'Yeah, but I can't be the guy who breaks my brother's heart,' Harrison said slowly. 'He thinks you're the one good thing in his life. I can't take that away from him.'

Flick pulled her hand loose from his grip, feeling a crushing weight settle on her chest

'Last night you said that you would never forget the look on your sister's face when she realised what had happened between you and Marc. I don't want to see that look in my brother's eyes, Flick. He's a mess at the moment. I spoke to Chloe this morning.' Harrison broke off to stare into the middle distance for a second. 'That's the problem with our family, no one ever talks. She's been worried about him for months, but she hasn't said anything. He's been stuffing up at work, causing problems, disappearing for days on end.'

Flick could see the pain and worry in his face, but all she could feel was pain. 'What does any of this have to do with me?' she asked. What she wanted to say was, 'Don't you love me? Doesn't last night mean anything to you?' But she realised now what the answer was. She'd been right to hesitate over telling him she loved him. It was her one small solace, that she hadn't utterly humiliated herself by throwing herself at his feet. A tiny shred of self-respect to wrap herself in.

'He said that letting you go was the biggest mistake of his life,' Harrison said flatly.

'He didn't let me go, Harrison,' she said, suddenly very weary. 'I walked away because I knew it was wrong, and it was never going to be right.'

Flick realised she had no more words. After last night, Harrison's decision felt like a punch in the face. She had been filled with so much hope this morning, so much expectation and anticipation. She turned away from him, moving towards the apartment building. She didn't want to talk anymore, not when it just meant more pain and rejection.

'I'm so dumb,' she thought. 'So stupid to think that he felt the same way as me. How could he walk away from me if he felt the same way?'

'Flick, please,' he called after her. 'You've got to understand—I can't steal my brother's happiness.'

Flick pushed through the double doors and into the foyer. She told herself that it was better to know now rather than later. But it didn't make the pain any easier to bear.

Harrison watched Flick walk away, his gut clenched with tension. He'd never felt so torn in his life. Everything in him wanted to chase after her and assure her it would all be all right. After all, he deserved happiness, too. He'd been miserable since Amanda's betrayal. Meeting Flick had been like switching the light on after too long in the dark.

But he stayed where he was, his feet rooted in family loyalty and an older brother's instinctive protection of his younger sibling. Marc and he had always gotten on well. His brother had been a light-hearted and generous kid, and he'd grown into a fun-loving, impulsive man. And then he'd met the two Scully sisters, and some of the light had gone out of him. The time he'd spent globetrotting was supposed to have helped cure his broken heart. But, clearly, it had not.

What if Marc was right? What if Flick was the love of his life? Didn't he owe it to his brother to step aside?

He shook his head, angry at his own ever-circling thoughts. He'd laid awake all night going over and over the same arguments. He'd had one night with Flick. With an older man's caution, he hesitated to call what he was feeling love. It sure as hell felt like it, but he was just emerging from a bitter divorce and he couldn't just throw aside the lessons he'd learnt over the past few months.

Could he?

So, where did that leave him? Nowhere. And seriously unhappy about it. And it was useless to deny the fear that gnawed deep inside his gut. What if Marc wooed Flick and won her over? Would he be able to sit back and watch his brother love her?

He ground his teeth together all the way back to the hotel, haunted by the lost look in her eyes as she registered his final words. He remembered what Marc had said: 'What if you found the one thing in your life that could make you happy, but you let it slip through your fingers?' He had a feeling those words were going to stay with him for a long time.

⌣

There was something going on with Flick. Michelle watched her sister hustle around the flat, tidying things that were already tidy, dusting, even cleaning the windows, for Pete's sake. Yep, something was definitely up.

But Michelle was too afraid to ask, too worried that she was the reason her sister was anxiously wiping down the fridge. She'd stuffed up, big time. And she'd scared herself, and Flick. She'd also humiliated herself in front of their downstairs neighbour, but that was a whole other ballgame.

She didn't know what to do to fix any of it. That was the problem, really. She'd felt nothing but lost since she'd come back from Australia, and even though yesterday had been terrifying, it didn't really change anything. She still had this empty feeling inside. When she'd been lying in hospital last night, she'd thought about calling Connor, telling him what had happened. Maybe he would drop everything and fly over to see her, he'd be so worried. She was so weak she'd even reached for the phone, but she knew that she couldn't do that to him. He had responsibilities now, and she wasn't the most important person in his world anymore.

There was the crash of something breaking from the kitchen, and then the low, vehement sound of Flick swearing. After a few moments, Michelle got up off the couch and came into the kitchen to find Flick sitting on the floor, just staring at the remains of her favourite coffee mug in front of her, the dustpan and broom lying unused to one side.

'Are you okay?' Michelle forced herself to ask.

Flick looked up at her. 'Why is falling in love so hard, Shelly? And why does it never work out for us?'

Michelle frowned, getting the distinct feeling Flick wasn't talking about her and Connor. Then she remembered the tall guy from out the front this morning. She'd been so preoccupied with her own problems she could barely remember his name.

She dropped to her knees so she was on the same eye level as her sister.

'Is this about that Harrison guy?' she asked hesitantly.

'He's Marc Lambert's brother, Shelly,' Flick stated baldly.

Michelle was shocked for a moment. 'Isn't he married?' She tried to keep the judgement from her voice, but it was there.

'Keep your knickers on, he's almost divorced,' Flick said snappily. 'And it doesn't matter anyway, because Marc has just turned up and Harrison has backed off at a million miles an hour.'

Her sister sounded utterly miserable underneath her anger.

'But you and Harrison haven't got something going on?' Michelle asked, confused. She'd seen no sign of a boyfriend in Flick's life. In fact, it was exactly the opposite. As far as she knew, Flick hadn't been out with anyone since she'd been living in New York.

'No. Yes. Sort of. It's complicated. And, like I said, it doesn't matter because now he's got this stupid idea that telling Marc how he feels about me would be "stealing Marc's happiness". Whatever that means,' Flick said.

Michelle winced as she began to see what sort of a mess Flick was in.

'Do you love him? Harrison, I mean,' she asked.

Flick picked up a chunk of the broken coffee mug and turned it over and over in her hands. At last she looked up, and Michelle saw tears in her eyes.

'More than anything, Shelly. I didn't even think it was possible to feel this way about someone so quickly. I mean, we've been working together for the past few months, but it's hardly been idyllic because he thought I was some sort of gold-digging tramp. But I used to watch him, the way he was with everyone else, and I could see that he was a good man. And yesterday we talked and we realised that we'd both been judging each other. And I realised that all this time I've been fighting this attraction to him ...'

Michelle coaxed the rest of it out of her sister over the next twenty minutes.

'Bloody men,' Flick finally said, rubbing a hand wearily across her tear-reddened eyes.

'Tell me about it,' Michelle said before she could help herself.

Flick shot her a sharp look, then nudged her with her toe. 'Go on, cough up. I've just spilled my guts all over the place.'

Michelle didn't know where to begin, but once she started talking, it all just poured out of her: how much she loved Connor, and how angry she'd been at him for sleeping with Lori, and how much she resented baby Maddy and how guilty that made her feel. And how she didn't have the courage to stay home and try to work things out, so instead she'd just come back here knowing that she would probably never meet anyone as amazing as Connor in her entire life.

By the time she was finished, she was crying so much there was snot on her face, and Flick was crying again, too. Flick had to go get some toilet paper from the bathroom because they were all out of tissues, and there were a few moments of sniffing and nose blowing as they both came down off their crying jag. Finally, Michelle met Flick's eyes and managed a small smile.

'How pathetic does this look, do you think?' she asked.

Flick shrugged a shoulder. 'On a scale of one to ten? About a twenty.'

They laughed, and Flick leant across and pulled her into a hug.

'I don't know what the answer is, Shelly. As you might have noticed, I suck at this love thing too. Maybe it's a Scully curse.'

'Easily fixed. No more men for the rest of my life,' Michelle announced grandly.

Flick raised an eyebrow at her. 'Yeah? Better avoid that cute Charlie guy from downstairs, then. He's got the hots for you,' she said, sweeping up the coffee mug at last and tipping the broken shards into the bin.

'Charlie? No way!' Michelle said, colouring up. But then she remembered the way he'd looked at her the few times they'd seen each other. She understood that was why she'd knocked on his door that time. Because she'd sensed he liked her, and part of her liked him, too.

She frowned, uncomfortable with the idea that she might be attracted to someone else. She'd loved Connor for so long, it felt wrong—really, really wrong—to be even thinking about someone else. Thoroughly unsettled, Michelle headed back to the couch to bury herself in a book and pretend Flick had never mentioned Charlie's name.

Chapter 8

When Flick arrived at work the next day Marc was waiting for her, sitting in the visitor's chair in her office, casually leafing through a magazine. He stood when he saw her, his eyes appreciative as they swept over her.

'You look great, Flick. I hate that corporate uniform, but you make it look good,' he said by way of greeting.

Flick just eyed him steadily before taking a deep breath and sliding into the seat behind her desk.

'My answer hasn't changed, Marc,' she said calmly.

He nodded, but she could see that he didn't really believe her.

'Have it your way. But there's no reason why we can't be friends, right? I'm going to stay in town with Harrison for a while, so we could hang out, maybe go see a few shows or go clubbing … ?'

Flick shook her head, hating the way her heart skipped a beat at just the mention of Harrison's name. 'We're not friends, Marc. We're exes, and for good reason. Now, if you don't mind, I've got work to do.'

He offered her a little bow from the waist. 'I'll leave you to it then.'

He was anything but resigned she realised as he shot her an intense look before exiting her office. She put her head in her hands. This was an impossible situation, and one she really didn't feel up to.

'Knock knock.'

Flick glanced up to see Jacobina in her doorway. 'Hi, JB. What's up?' she asked, feigning lightness.

'Got a headache, boss lady?' Jacobina asked. Flick realised she must have seen her with her head in her hands.

'I've just got a bad case of Lambert-itis,' Flick said without thinking.

Jacobina cocked her head to one side. 'So that was the infamous Marc Lambert I just saw leaving your office. How about that,' she said, speculation gleaming in her eye.

'What do you mean, infamous?' Flick asked, surprised.

'Girlfriend, you need to spend more time in the staff room. He's the original jet setting playboy, that one. The grapevine says he's been in the Bahamas for the past few months, working in the hotel there. Only he spent more time working the female staff members, if you know what I mean,' Jacobina said.

Flick shifted in her chair, uncomfortable with gossiping. She knew what it was like to have people spreading rumours about you.

'You steer clear of that one, okay?' Jacobina advised sagely.

'Yes, mother,' Flick said.

'Good girl. Leo asked me to let you know he's called a meeting for nine-thirty. Wants to update all the managers on the renovations or something. Cool?'

'I'll be there,' Flick assured her.

Once she was alone, Flick shuffled papers around on her desk but all she could think about was seeing Harrison. He was bound to be at the meeting. How was she going to cope with sitting opposite him and pretending nothing had happened?

She had her answer soon enough: badly.

The moment he walked in the room she felt as though every cell in her body had suddenly switched into overdrive. Her heart started to race, and she could feel her breath coming faster and shallower. She shot a glance across at the smooth planes and angles of his face, and felt her heart squeeze painfully in her chest. Then his eyes met hers, and she made herself look away before she hurled herself across the table and pleaded with him to love her the way she loved him.

If only she could forget how it had felt to lie in his arms, to kiss his lips. Abruptly she pulled her attention back to the paperwork in front of her. She had to stop thinking like this. It wasn't getting her anywhere, and it wasn't making things any easier.

Harrison realised he was gripping his pen so hard that it was digging into his palm. Making a conscious effort, he relaxed his hand and let the pen drop onto the conference table. Flick looked tired and hurt. Snap. They were a matched set—but he already knew that. Not for the first time in the last forty-eight hours, he wished that things were different. But Marc had set up residence in the penthouse, and declared his intention to stay put until he'd won Flick over. It was like a custom-made, exquisite form of torture, listening to his brother talk about his tactics to woo her, and then pretending to look interested as he reported back his conversations with Flick.

Harrison loved his brother, but it made acid burn in his belly to think of him winning Flick. She was his. Every fibre of his being said so.

So why was he bowing out, when she was sitting there, his for the taking? As if in answer to his question, the door to the conference room opened and Marc walked in. He flashed a charming smile and slid into an empty seat.

'Sorry I'm late. Got held up,' he explained quickly, his eyes automatically zeroing in on Flick.

Harrison could feel Leo looking to him, startled to see Marc at the table. As well he might be—Marc had no position or authority at Lassiter's Towers. He was supposed to be based in the Lassiter's Nautilus Reef in the Bahamas. Yet here he was, pulling up a chair with the other executives.

He knew why Marc was here, of course—it was all about pursuing Flick. But this was not the place for it. Equally, he wasn't about to humiliate his brother by pointing out as much in front of the hotel's senior staff. Instead, he gave Leo a small reassuring nod, indicating he would take care of the situation after the meeting.

Leo resumed his rundown on the renovation, and Harrison forced himself to look away from the intensity in his brother's eyes as he watched Flick. That Marc loved Flick he had no doubt.

Sometime later, the sound of paper rustling jolted him back to the present, and Harrison realised that the meeting was over. He had no recall of any of it, but no one was staring at him strangely so he figured he'd gotten away with it. He frowned, disliking being so out of control. He never lost concentration at work. Not until meeting Flick, anyway.

The managers were filing out. Flick shot him a look as she passed by, her mahogany eyes haunted. He almost reached out to stop her from leaving. Almost.

But Marc was there, too, and he didn't think he could talk to Flick without revealing himself. Not just at the moment, anyway. Realising Marc was about to head out the door, he pulled himself together.

'Marc, can I have a word before you disappear?' he asked.

Marc hung back obligingly, his expression relaxed and casual.

'Would you mind closing the door?' Harrison suggested, knowing Marc wouldn't want what he had to say to be overheard by anyone else.

Marc shrugged and pushed the door closed, leaning against it negligently.

'Let me guess, I'm in for a telling off,' he said.

Harrison shook his head. 'Not at all. But I just thought we should clear up a few things. If you want to attend staff meetings, you need to be on staff, Marc. It's not on to just waltz in and out like that.'

Marc frowned and tossed his head. 'Who cares if I'm here or not? Leo? Maybe someone should remind him who signs his pay cheques.'

Harrison narrowed his eyes. Since when had his brother developed this 'ruling classes' attitude? It certainly hadn't been present the last time they'd spent significant time together. But then, that had been some time ago, at least a couple of years thanks to their mutual hectic travel schedules.

'I care, for starters. And it's not fair to Felicity for you to use the workplace to pursue her, either. Keep it out of work hours, Marc,' Harrison advised stiffly.

Marc smirked. 'All's fair in love and war, mate,' he said.

'So you love this woman?' Harrison challenged.

'I do. Why do you think I'm here when I could be in the Bahamas getting a tan?'

'Then give her the respect of allowing her time and space to adjust to you being here. If you love her, that's the least you can do.'

It was Marc's turn to narrow his eyes.

'You're taking a bit of an interest, aren't you? What's it to you?'

'I love her, too.' The words were on the tip of Harrison's tongue, but he couldn't say them. Instead, he held his brother's eye for a long moment before looking away.

'I'm your brother. I want you to be happy. I just don't think this is the right way to go about getting what you want.'

Marc rolled his eyes, but he hooked his foot around the leg of a chair to pull it out, and flopped into it.

'Okay, hit me—what should I do?'

Harrison flinched, everything in him baulking at advising his brother on how to romance Flick.

'In case you hadn't noticed, I'm getting a divorce,' he said evasively. 'I don't think you want my advice where women are concerned.'

'The least you can do is give me a job, then, so I can see her legitimately at work every day. That way Leo can't get all bunged up over me attending meetings.'

'I can't just create a position out of thin air, Marc,' Harrison said, exasperated by his brother's attitude. 'This isn't Monopoly we're playing here, these are real hotels we're talking about.'

'You sound just like Mum and Dad. Spare me the lecture. If you can't find me something to do, fine. It's no skin off my nose,' Marc said, pushing himself up out of the chair.

Once he was alone, Harrison let out a gust of air and ran a distracted hand through his hair. This was an impossible situation. He was trying to do the right thing, but he felt dishonest. And, worse, he felt as though he was letting Flick down every time he looked at her and remembered the magic of that night.

Michelle raised her hand to knock on Charlie's door then hesitated. She wasn't even sure what she wanted to say. 'Thank you and sorry for being so obnoxious last time I visited'? But then she remembered what Flick had said about him liking her and she suddenly felt overwhelmed by self-consciousness and uncertainty. She didn't want Charlie to like her like that. She wasn't interested in anyone except for Connor.

Shaking her head at her own stupidity, Michelle swivelled on her heel, ready to retreat. Only to find Charlie standing behind her, key in hand, a faint smile curving his mouth.

'Michelle. Good to see you home,' he said.

Michelle could feel herself blushing. 'I was just coming to say thanks for everything,' she explained hurriedly.

'It's cool. Happy to be of help,' he said. 'Just glad to see you up and about, no harm done.'

'And, just so you know, I'm not usually like this,' Michelle said.

Where had that come from? What did she care what he thought of her, after all? She barely knew him.

'Anyway, I've got stuff to do,' she said, backing away.

'How's the head?' he asked before she could go.

'Um, good. A few stitches, but the doctor said they'll just dissolve on their own.'

Michelle automatically lifted the heavy weight of her hair off the back of her neck to show him, and he stepped forward to inspect the doctor's handiwork. She could smell him, a mixture of fresh baked bread and some sort of sporty deodorant. His fingers were warm on her neck as he smoothed her hair further out of the way so he could get a better look. She kept her eyes on the ground, a little afraid of looking at him when he was standing so close.

'Lucky it's on your hair line, eh?' he said, at last letting her hair fall back down. 'Otherwise you'd have a big shaved patch.'

'Yeah. Lucky I didn't crack my head open,' she said, taking an instinctive step away from him.

His eyes followed the movement, and his lip quirked a little to one side.

'Well, I'd better go get changed for work,' he said.

Michelle just nodded stupidly as he waved a hand at her and let himself into his apartment. She was left feeling slightly put out as the door closed on him. For some reason, that hadn't gone quite the way she'd expected. Although she wasn't quite sure what she'd expected either.

She shrugged, digging her hands into the back pockets of her jeans. She had her foot on the first stair tread when his apartment door opened again and he appeared in the doorway.

'Hey, Michelle, I was thinking—would you like to go to a movie or something sometime?' he asked casually.

Michelle froze in place. He was asking her out. What should she say? He was standing in his doorway, waiting expectantly. She liked him; he was a nice guy. But she wasn't in the market for a boyfriend. Before she could stop herself, the words had popped out her mouth.

'I'm not looking for a boyfriend right now,' she said.

She felt a tide of hot colour rushing up her

neck and into her cheeks. Why had she said that? She was such a geek.

'Sure. I just meant as friends,' Charlie said easily. Even though she hadn't thought it was possible, the heat in her cheeks intensified.

'Right. Um, well, yeah. A movie sounds good,' she managed to choke out.

'Cool. Tonight sound okay? I don't get a night off for another week after that.'

'Sure. Tonight's good,' Michelle agreed.

Then Charlie smiled and nodded, and disappeared back into his apartment. Michelle was left alone in the foyer, just her and her embarrassment. Why had she listened to Flick about Charlie liking her? Now he probably thought she was some sort of deluded loser who imagined everybody was in love with her. Rolling her eyes at her own stupidity, Michelle trudged upstairs.

Flick came home at the usual time, and Michelle was glad she'd made dinner when she saw how worn out and miserable her sister looked.

'Crappy day?' she asked as she slid a bowl of risotto in front of Flick.

'Just a bit. Marc Lambert seems to think he only has to ask the right number of times before I fall at his feet,' she said tiredly. 'He keeps looking at me with this intense, puppy dog look, and I feel awful saying no, but I am absolutely not interested.'

'What about Harrison? Was he there?' Michelle asked cautiously.

'He acts like nothing ever happened between us. I'm beginning to think that I just imagined that night,' Flick said glumly.

'But you didn't. You stayed up talking till nearly four in the morning. You said it yourself—you fell in love that night, Flick.'

'But clearly he didn't, otherwise he wouldn't just step back like this and let Marc do his thing. Would he?' Flick looked at her, desperate for reassurance.

'Ask him,' Michelle suggested boldly.

Flick blanched. 'Right, and humiliate myself even more.'

'At least you'll know. Then you can move on, or you can fight for this thing between you two. Wouldn't that be better than living in limbo land?' Michelle asked.

Flick poked at her risotto, deep in thought. 'Maybe.'

Michelle cleared her throat, aware that she needed to tell Flick about her date.

'Um, I'm going out to the movies tonight. With Charlie,' she announced.

Flick blinked with surprise, then she gave Michelle a little nudge with her elbow. 'You're a fast worker, aren't you?'

'It's not like that. We're just going as friends,' Michelle said.

'Riiiighhht,' Flick said, eyebrows wiggling up and down suggestively.

Michelle made an annoyed noise and concentrated on her risotto. 'We are, okay? When he asked me I said I wasn't looking for a boyfriend, and he said it was just as friends.'

'Bull. He likes you, Michelle. Why else would he ask you out?'

Michelle frowned, thinking about it. Maybe Flick was right. Unless he felt sorry for her, and that was why he was asking her out. She hated the idea that he'd asked her out of pity. But she didn't have time to brood on it because he arrived just as she was putting her bowl in the sink.

'I'll do the dishes, off you go,' Flick insisted, shooing her out the door.

And so Michelle found herself walking down to the cinemaplex with Charlie. It was cold out, so she was well wrapped up in a woolly hat and scarf and a thick coat, and they dodged puddles of snow and sludge as they picked their way along the pavement. It was strange being out with a boy who wasn't Connor. She kept shooting little glances across at his face as they walked, trying to work out what he was thinking. It hadn't been like that with Connor. It had been comfortable, familiar. She frowned. Charlie had asked her out as a friend, nothing more. She had to stop thinking about that stuff.

He kept up a steady stream of questions and chat as they walked, and she heard about his job and his family, and the dog he'd left behind in Toronto and how he was planning a trip home in the next few months, if he could get the time off. By the time they got to the cinema, she'd relaxed a bit and told him a bit about her family back home in Australia. They studied the marquee at the cinemaplex, but neither of them could find anything they liked the sound of. Charlie suggested they go get coffee and cake instead, and soon they were ensconced in a booth in a coffee shop, steaming mugs of hot chocolate in front of them, and a whopping great slice of cake sitting between them.

'There's no way we can eat all that,' Michelle said, eyeing the chocolate monstrosity warily.

She was wrong. By the time they'd argued over who got to eat most of the icing, and whether ice-cream or cream was the best accompaniment for cake, the huge slice had been reduced to a few crumbs in a puddle of cream. They both had another hot chocolate each, and then Michelle realised with astonishment that almost three hours had passed. Charlie was good company, light-hearted and fun, but also sincere when he was talking about things that mattered to him. She liked the dimple in his cheek, and enjoyed seeing it flash when she said something that made him laugh. He had nice brown eyes, and a cute way of lifting up one eyebrow when he was having her on.

Before she knew it, they were standing on the landing outside her apartment, saying goodbye. Some of her earlier awkwardness returned now that they were alone in the darkened hallway, and Michelle felt butterflies dancing in her belly as she glanced up at him.

'Well, thanks Michelle, I had fun,' he said. Then he leaned forward to drop a casual kiss on her cheek. Clapping a hand on her arm in a brotherly fashion, he headed off down the stairs.

Michelle stared after him, feeling decidedly miffed that he hadn't even tried to kiss her. She hadn't wanted him to, mind. But he could have at least tried.

Flick stared at her reflection in the bathroom mirror. She was turning into a hag. Many more sleepless nights and she was going to need a face lift. She dabbed concealer under her eyes and checked the effect. Now she looked like a panda. Sighing, she splashed cold water on her face and used a tissue to wipe the concealer off. She'd never been much good at covering up with make-up. If anyone asked, she'd say she was coming down with the flu. It might even be true, the way she was feeling right now.

She read over some new literature from head office while she ate breakfast, deliberately trying to distract herself from thoughts of Harrison and Marc. It was useless—she just kept reading the same paragraph over and over as she wondered what Harrison was doing right now, whether he was thinking about her, when she'd see him at work. 'Pathetic, Scully,' she thought. 'You need to get a grip.'

Her workday got off to an even worse start when she arrived to find Marc waiting in her office again. He was wearing jeans and a casual blue wool jumper that exactly matched his eyes. In contrast to her, he looked well-rested and perky.

'Good morning. I brought you a bagel,' he said, sliding a bakery bag across the table towards her.

Flick stared at the bag, feeling momentarily overwhelmed by the situation. She sat in her chair and regarded Marc for a moment before speaking.

'The answer's still no, Marc,' she said wearily. How long was this going to go on?

'I understand. But it won't stop me loving you,' Marc said. His face was very serious as he watched her. 'I've never stopped loving you, Flick.'

Flick shot a nervous glance over his shoulder. He hadn't bothered to modify his voice, and the last thing she wanted was for anyone to overhear the conversation.

She lowered her own voice. 'Marc, this has to stop. No more morning visits. I'm a manager here; I have staff. I can't afford to have people talking about why one of the heirs to the Lambert empire keeps hanging around in my office.'

'I'm not ashamed of us, Flick,' he said.

'There is no "us", Marc. Please believe that.'

Suddenly Jacobina appeared in her doorway.

'Here are those papers you asked for,' she said, winking one eye crazily. Flick stared at her blankly, then realised that Jacobina was signalling for her to go along with her story.

'Thank you, JB. Have you got time to go over them now?' Flick improvised.

'Absolutely.'

Both of them turned to stare at Marc and he shrugged a shoulder. 'Never let it be said that I can't take a hint. Have a good day, Flick,' he said before ducking out of the office.

Jacobina closed the door after him and eyed Flick narrowly. 'Okay, what's going on? Why does Mr Playboy keep cornering you in your office? And why do you look like you're about to chew off your arm every time he does it, just so you can escape? And did I hear him just call you Flick? What kind of a name is that?'

Flick took a deep breath and answered the safest question first.

'It's a family nickname. Everyone used to call me it back home.'

'Everyone? Including Marc Lambert?' Jacobina fished.

Flick's shoulders sagged. Jacobina had a determined glint in her eye. There was no way she was leaving without something.

'Marc and I knew each in Australia. I worked for the Lassiter's hotel near home.'

'Yeah, yeah, Lassiter's Erinsborough. I knew that. But that still doesn't explain why Marc Lambert is hanging around your office every morning, bringing you bagels,' Jacobina said.

Flick stared at the incriminating bagel. Bloody Marc and his persistence! She'd been so careful not to do anything that would cause gossip or talk in the hotel. If word of her past relationship with Marc got out, it would spread like wildfire. She hated the idea of being the butt of gossip again. Just the thought of it made her sick to the stomach with anxiety.

'I can keep a secret, don't worry,' Jacobina encouraged gently. 'Plus, no offence, but you look like you need a friend.'

Flick was surprised to feel tears in her eyes. 'Damn it,' she swore, opening drawers in her desk looking for a tissue.

'Here,' Jacobina said, offering a freshly laundered handkerchief.

Flick sniffed and wiped at her eyes and then finally met Jacobina's patient gaze.

'Marc was once engaged to my sister,' she began. Jacobina's eyes rounded, and they pretty much stayed round as Flick told her sorry tale, leaving out her current feelings for Harrison. The less said about that, the better.

'So what are you going to do?' Jacobina asked when Flick had finally wound down.

'Wait him out. He won't believe me when I say there's no chance, so I'm just going to keep saying it until he does.'

'I meant about Harrison. What are you going to do about Harrison?' Jacobina asked.

Flick stared at her, genuinely gobsmacked. 'What?'

'Oh, come on, do you think I'm blind or something? First you guys were hissing and spitting at each other every time you were in the same room, next he's screaming out the door with you because your sister was hurt. I know when love is in the air,' Jacobina said.

Flick bit her lip and nodded, realising how obvious it must have been. It also explained the searching looks Leo had been giving her lately.

'Harrison and I were over before we even got started. He won't step on Marc's toes now that he's turned up saying that he still loves me.'

'What a load of baloney!' Jacobina exploded. 'That man doesn't love you! He's been doing the horizontal mambo with every girl he could get his hands on all throughout the Bahamas, and it wouldn't surprise me if he was putting the hard word on the girls here as well. He's not in love with you, Flick. Maybe he just wants the one thing that he can't have. But he's not in love with you.'

Flick stared at her friend, realising that she'd just articulated something that had been at the back of her mind since Marc had arrived.

'When I broke up with him the first time he wouldn't take no for an answer, either. I don't think he's missed out on much in life,' she said dryly.

'Do him good to miss out for once, from what I've seen,' Jacobina judged.

Flick frowned, remembering the Marc she used to know. 'He wasn't always like this. He was really sweet and funny when I first met him. But he doesn't know what he wants. That's his real problem. It even happened with me and Steph: first he wanted her then he wanted me. Then it all went pear-shaped. He didn't want to work in the hotel chain, he wanted to travel—I guess he's just a bit of a lost spirit,' she finished lamely.

Jacobina made a rude noise. 'He's spoilt, that's what it is. He's had everything handed to him on a silver platter, and he doesn't want any of it.'

Flick realised that they were moving from confession into character assassination, and no matter how she felt about Marc personally, she wasn't about to tear him apart with one of his employees.

'Listen, JB, you've been great, but there's not a hell of a lot anyone can do about any of this,' Flick said. 'Thanks for listening though.'

'You hang in there. And next time he comes around annoying you, give me a buzz. I'll be happy to bounce him out of your office.'

Jacobina gave her a squeeze on the shoulder before she exited. Flick stared after her, momentarily wondering if she should call her back and remind her that everything she'd just said was strictly private and confidential. But then she remembered Jacobina's gentle comment that she could keep a secret. She didn't need to be told to keep Flick's confidences private.

Flick was forced to rethink her assessment when she passed by two chambermaids later that afternoon. As soon as they spotted her they stopped talking and ducked their heads. Flick could feel their eyes following her as she walked the length of the corridor. She frowned, wondering what they could possibly have been talking about that they would stop when she appeared. She wasn't even their boss—that was Sadie. Paranoia nibbled at the edge of her consciousness, but she pushed it aside. But half an hour later, when she passed the door to the staff room, she was left in no doubt that the word was out. She was about to enter the room when she realised she'd collected a bit of gum on the sole of her shoe. She leant against the wall to pry it off, and the conversation from inside the staff room filtered out to her.

'... and she was bridesmaid and everything! Can you imagine doing that to your sister?'

Flick blanched, and anxiety clutched in the pit of her stomach. 'Please, no,' she begged silently. 'Please let them be talking about someone else.' It was a thin hope, and it was dashed when she entered the staff room and two of the admin clerks abruptly stopped talking. She knew then. Jacobina had broken her confidence. A cold fury gripped her. Coming to New York had been her fresh start. And she'd proven herself here. Now her past was rising up from the dead, and people were going to be only too happy to pick over the bones. That was something she'd learnt last time around—people loved to talk about other people's misfortunes, and sit in judgement over their mistakes.

Without even bothering to pretend she hadn't heard, Flick did an abrupt about-face and struck out down the corridor. She steamed into the administration area and flung open the door to the front reception area. Jacobina was restocking the printer tray, and Flick eyed her coldly.

'Jacobina, I'd like to see you in my office, please,' she said.

Jacobina looked up, frowning at the tone in Flick's voice. Flick didn't wait to see whether the other woman was following her, she simply swivelled on her heel and marched to her office. She stood there, arms crossed, as Jacobina approached a worried expression on her face.

'Hey, what's up?' she asked, looking uncertain.

Flick kicked the door shut and turned to face her friend. 'Who did you tell?'

'What?'

'You heard me, who did you tell? You just couldn't resist it, could you? Having a nice little gossip at my expense. I trusted you, JB! I've kept all that stuff about Marc to myself for all the time I've been here, and I trusted you to keep my secret!'

Jacobina's worried expression cleared to be replaced by one of righteous anger.

'And I kept it, thank you very much. If you think I ran around telling everybody about you and Marc, you've got another thing coming. I wouldn't do that to you, Felicity. You're my friend!' she said.

Flick wavered, suddenly unsure. But those women had been talking about her, she knew they had. There was no way they could know unless … Flick sat down in her chair with a thump.

Marc. It had to be. Only he and Harrison knew the truth, and Harrison would never talk about it. Suddenly she knew with absolute certainty that Marc had been behind the rumour. She could see exactly what he thought to gain from it—the two of them linked in shame once again. It had worked once before, after all.

'JB, I owe you an apology,' Flick said, her voice quavering with anger. 'I just realised who's been talking.'

Jacobina still looked defiant and hurt, but Flick realised she had a right to be. She stood, crossing to the door.

'What are you going to do?' Jacobina said as Flick pulled it open.

'What I should have done when Marc first turned up on my doorstep,' Flick said with determination.

Chapter 9

*F*lick knocked briskly on the door to the penthouse suite, her jaw set. She was determined to get through to Marc, to end this thing. And she was angry, very angry, that he had put her in the position of being the subject of gossip and rumour again. This had been her clean start, her break with the past. And now people were going to look at her and judge her again, just like back home. Marc had taken away her chance to put the past behind her, and she could never forgive him for that. Never mind that he'd also taken away her chance to form a relationship with his brother, too. That was a deep, dark hole she couldn't bear to examine just now.

He answered the door almost immediately, his eyes lighting up with expectation when he saw her.

'Flick. Come in,' he said, standing aside to let her pass. She shot him a hard look and strode briskly into the suite.

'This won't take long. I know what you did, Marc. I wanted to thank you face-to-face for dumping me in it again. As if I didn't have enough fingers pointing and judgemental looks back home.'

Marc raised his eyebrows and held up his hands palm out. 'Whoa there, Flick. I'm not sure exactly what I'm supposed to have done here, but whatever it is, I'm sure we can work it out,' he said.

'You told someone about you and me Marc, don't deny it. Half the staff are talking about it. No one here knows that we used to go out—no one except you, me and Harrison.'

'Then Harrison must have told someone,' Marc shrugged, leaning against the wall casually, one hand sliding into the pocket of his jeans.

Flick narrowed her eyes at him. When had Marc become a liar?

'Harrison would never stoop this low,' she said with absolute certainty. 'He's one of the most moral men I've ever met.'

Marc frowned. 'How heart warming.

Remind me to tell him you hold him in such high esteem.'

Flick felt a give away blush rising in her cheeks, and she lifted a hand to push her fringe out of the way, shielding her face for a few vital seconds.

'I've worked with Harrison for more than two months, Marc. I've seen the way he operates. You're the only person who has anything to gain from spreading rumours about us.'

She held his eye, and Marc finally glanced away. Flick's blood boiled.

'I knew it! I can't believe you would do this to me! You say you love me—what a great way to show it! Do you have any idea how hard I've worked to earn people's respect here? I have gone beyond the call of duty. I have worked my guts out. And now you bring all that … crap from back home with you.'

To her dismay, Flick felt tears pricking at the back of her eyes. She gritted her teeth, determined not to cry. But Marc picked that she was upset and he started forward, one hand reaching out to comfort her.

'Flick,' he began, but she slapped his hand away.

'Don't you dare try to touch me. You're a rat, Marc. Did you really think that spreading nasty stories about me would give me no choice but to turn to you? Did you really think that it would be like old times, and I'd come running to you for comfort?'

Something flickered behind his eyes, and she realised that that was exactly what he had thought. She drew herself up to her full height and straightened her shoulders.

'I should have told you this straight out the other day. I'm in love with someone else, Marc, so there is absolutely no chance of us ever getting back together,' she said.

She was shaking with anger and determination, her body slightly angled forward as she blasted him with the truth.

'Who is he?' Marc demanded instantly, his lip curling into a sneer. 'Who's this Mr Wonderful, then? And if he's so great, how come you haven't mentioned him before?'

'We're not together, if that's what you're asking. But it doesn't matter. Meeting this person has made me realise what real love is. I'd rather be alone than settle for anything less.'

She started for the door, but Marc stepped in her path, hands coming up to grab her upper arms. He towered over her, his blue eyes intense.

'Don't do this to me. I need you, Flick. You have no idea … I need you to be happy again,' he said, his voice vibrating with the intensity of his feelings.

Flick shook her head slowly and shrugged herself free from his grip.

'It's not my job to make you happy, Marc. Find your own way, be a grown-up for a change.'

She pushed passed him, and he let her go. In the lift, she took deep breaths to dispel the last of her anger. She was just regaining some sort of equilibrium when the lift stopped on the executive floor and the doors slid open to reveal Harrison. He frowned when he saw her and stepped briskly into the lift.

'What's wrong?' he asked immediately, his eyes scanning her face. 'What's happened?'

Flick stared up at him, wishing with all her heart that Harrison felt the same way that she did. How could she feel so strongly for him, yet he remained unmoved by the time they spent together?

'I'm fine,' she shrugged. She wanted all of him, not just his polite concern, or misplaced guilt.

'Flick,' he said, his tone heavy with disbelief.

'It doesn't matter, Harrison. And really, it's none of your business, is it?' she said.

He tilted his chin, almost as though he was withstanding a blow. Then he nodded.

'No, you're right.'

They completed the rest of the trip to the foyer in silence, and all the while Flick wondered how long it was going to take for her heart to stop aching every time she saw him.

Harrison followed Flick with his eyes as she exited the lift and crossed the foyer to the reception desk. Her shoulders drooped a little as she relaxed her guard, and he felt a stab of frustration and regret. This was crazy. He wanted to be with her. They'd connected. They were drawn to each other. And the reasons for being apart seemed murkier every day. Marc might love Flick—but clearly she didn't feel the same way. She certainly hadn't greeted him with open arms. Which meant she could still be his—if he was prepared to stand up and claim her. If he hadn't left it too late. And if he hadn't hurt her too much.

It wasn't even a question, he realised. There was no room for debate. Decisive, he turned back to the lift bank and stabbed the call button. Watching the floor indicator impatiently, he willed the lift to return to the ground floor. Finally the doors slid open, and he stepped aside as a handful of guests spilled out into the foyer. Circling around them, he swiped his pass card in the security slot and pressed the button for the penthouse floor.

He realised something was wrong the moment he exited the lift. Even though the door to the suite was closed, he could hear the sound of smashing glass clearly. He covered the distance between the lift and the front door in two strides, and swiped his way into the room. Marc spun on his heel to face him as he entered, his eyes wild as he held up a whisky bottle. A number of smashed tumblers lay near the opposite wall.

'Hey ya big bro! Come to have a drink with me?' he asked.

Harrison eyed his brother cautiously. Was he drunk? What was going on?

'What's going on?' he asked calmly.

'Nothing much, nothing important—except she's in love with someone else,' Marc revealed.

Harrison froze. 'What did you say?' he demanded.

'Flick. She's in love with someone else. Said she'd never realised what real love was until she met him. Great, huh?'

Despite his brother's anger and pain, Harrison felt a band of tension relax from around his chest. She loved him. Despite his stupidity in the way he'd handled this difficult situation, she loved him. He hadn't lost her; it wasn't too late. There was still a chance for them to make it work.

All of his own uncertainties dropped away. This was right, this thing between him and Flick. Marc was just going to have to understand.

'She's not even with this idiot, either, but she won't give me a chance to make things up to her,' Marc ranted. He lifted the whisky bottle to his mouth then stared at it long and hard before placing it down on the coffee table with a thunk. Sighing heavily, he sank down onto the lounge and put his head in his hands.

'I have to get this right, Harry. I have to make things right,' he said.

Harrison could hear the pain and confusion in his brother's voice, but he knew that he'd put off the moment of truth for too long.

'Marc, I need to tell you something,' he said, moving to sit opposite his brother. 'Before you got here, Flick and I were at each other's throats like cat and dog. But then something happened, and we realised that maybe all our problems were about liking each other too much, rather than not enough. We spent some time together, and something happened.'

Marc lifted his head slowly, a dawning understanding in his eyes.

'You're the guy. You're the guy she's in love with,' he guessed.

Harrison nodded. 'Yeah. And I'm in love with her, too, Marc. I've tried to stand back and let you take your shot, but I can't do it. I've been looking for someone like Flick all my life.'

Marc's face crumpled with disbelief, and he recoiled back on the couch.

'I can't believe this.'

'It just happened, Marc. No one planned for things to go this way,' Harrison said.

Marc exploded up out of the couch and took a couple of hasty paces across the room, almost as though his anger and disbelief wouldn't let him remain still.

'Let me get this straight. You just happened to fall in love with the woman I've spent the last three years trying to forget. That just accidentally happened, did it, Harry?'

Marc's eyes were wild, the cords in his neck standing out with rage.

'Like I said, nobody planned for it to happen, but it has. I know you feel like Flick is the only good thing in your life at the moment —'

'Jesus! Can you hear yourself, Harry? Don't try and rationalise this situation to me. You're sitting there telling me you're going to trip off into the sunset with the woman I love. And you expect me to just goddamn accept that?!' Marc demanded.

Harrison stared at his brother, aware that anything he said right now was only likely to inflame the situation. There was instability in Marc, an edginess that was new. He'd registered it ever since Marc had turned up.

'Maybe we should talk about this later,' he said, standing.

Marc made a furious noise and lunged across the room, straight-arming Harrison in the chest. Taken unawares, Harrison staggered backwards into the wall. Marc came at him again, teeth bared, face hard. Harrison neatly sidestepped the approach, using Marc's forward momentum to knock him off balance. Marc lurched to the side, then quickly regained his balance and whirled to face his brother again.

Harrison deliberately relaxed his stance and spread his hands, palm up, in front of himself. 'I'm not fighting you, Marc. And I'm not trying to steal anything from you, either. Flick is her own person, she makes her own choices. And you've been gone from her life for over three years.'

Marc shook his head. 'You knew how I felt about her. I told you, that time we went skiing. I told you what she meant to me, how I couldn't forget her.'

Harrison nodded, acknowledging Marc's point. 'I remember that night. It's the reason why Flick and I were at each other's throats for a long time. But it didn't stop me from falling in love with her, Marc.'

Marc stared at him for a long moment then he pivoted on his heel and crossed to the floor to ceiling window. He stood there, staring out at the Manhattan skyline for a long time. Harrison watched the tense line of his brother's shoulders, guilt sitting like a rock in his belly. He knew how he would feel if Marc had succeeded in wooing Flick back. He'd be angry, too.

After a long time, Marc turned back to face him. His face was set into hard lines.

'You have to choose, Harry. You want Flick, you take her. But you're not my brother anymore,' he said coldly.

Harrison flinched. Marc couldn't be serious. It was anger talking, anger and dis-appointment.

'Marc, I know this has taken you by surprise—' he began, but Marc held up a hand and shook his head.

'I mean it. I'm not going to sit back while you build a life with her, Harry. I won't be a part of it. So you make your choice—her or me.'

'This is ridiculous,' Harrison said, hands flinging wide in frustration. 'Once you've calmed down you'll realise we can work this out.'

Marc moved closer, and Harrison realised there were tears in his eyes.

'You are my brother, and I love you with all my soul, but you can't have us both,' he said, his voice low and very serious.

Harrison lifted an arm, wanting to comfort him. But Marc shied away.

'Her or me, Harry,' he said, then he turned on his heel and walked through to his bedroom.

Michelle rested the wooden spoon against the side of the mixing bowl and shook out her aching hand. Charlie arched an eyebrow mockingly.

'Too tough for you, Aussie girl? Bit of cookie batter wiped you out?' he teased.

Michelle poked her tongue out at him.

'You put too many chocolate bits in,' she said. 'It's like cement.'

Charlie put down the icing bag he was holding and crossed to check the bowl. Grabbing the spoon, he churned the batter a few times then gave Michelle a conciliatory smile.

'Okay, it's a little chunky—but it'll be worth it, don't worry,' he assured her.

He was standing to one side of her, so close that she could feel the heat radiating off his body. When she looked up into his eyes, she could see flecks of green and gold among the brown. The more she looked at him, she realised, the cuter he got. And the more she wondered if he was ever going to kiss her.

Like now, for instance. There was no one else home. They'd been hanging out together all day, since she had a study day and he had the day off work. They'd watched a video, gone for a walk, and now they were making cookies from Charlie's secret recipe. And she was just about ready to scream with frustration.

Sometimes she was sure he liked her, 'liked her' liked her not just 'friends' liked her. When they were picking the video in the shop, for instance, she'd turned around and caught him watching her with this particular look in his eye. Her breath had caught in her throat for a second, and she'd felt really self-conscious. But then something else would happen, like the way he just casually shoved her off the couch when they got home, so she had to sit on the floor to watch the video while he stretched out on the sofa. Nobody who liked a girl would do that to her, right?

But then she realised that sitting like that his face was sort of right next to hers, and if she just turned her head a little they'd be kissing. So what did that mean? She was going a little crazy trying to work it all out, and also trying to work out if she wanted him to kiss her or not.

He was fun to be around. And he was pretty cute, too. She definitely liked spending time with him. But she still thought about Connor a lot. Too much, if she really was interested in Charlie, surely?

But if he kissed her, things might all just fall into place. She'd know whether she liked him or not, and things would be a lot less confusing and uncertain.

She shot him a look out of the corners of her eyes then deliberately leaned a little closer to him. Her arm brushed his chest, and for a second she felt the slow, regular thump of his heartbeat. How could he be so calm when her heart was pounding out of control, like she'd just run a race?

Charlie glanced down at her, and she saw a flash of awareness in his eyes before he stepped away and went back to icing the cookies.

'Just a few more minutes, I promise,' he said, encouraging her to start stirring again.

Michelle pressed her lips together. Maybe she was imagining all this stuff. Maybe because Flick had told her Charlie liked her, she was projecting a whole bunch of stuff onto him that wasn't even there.

The sound of a key in the door had her walking into the front hall as her sister entered. Flick looked pale and tired, and she dumped her backpack in the hallway with a decidedly lacklustre air.

'You okay?' Michelle asked.

Flick shrugged. 'Headache. Leo sent me home.'

She trudged through into the living room then registered Charlie's presence.

'Oh, hi Charlie. You trying to make me and Michelle fat or something with all these biscuits?' she asked.

'They say food is the way to a good woman's heart,' Charlie said lightly. Unseen around the corner, Michelle pulled a frustrated face. What was that supposed to mean? Was he talking about her heart, or was he just mucking around again?

Flick gave a little half-smile and wandered through into her bedroom. Michelle went to follow her, but Flick was already swinging the door shut. Michelle pulled up short.

'Hmph,' she said to herself, shrugging.

'Leave her to it, Shelly. And come back and finish these cookies. You're the worst apprentice chef in the world,' Charlie said from behind her.

'Maybe I have a bad teacher, did you think about that?' she said as she headed back past him towards the kitchen.

To her surprise, she felt a firm spank on her bum. She turned, wide-eyed, to stare at him.

'Don't look at me like that,' he said. 'Chef training gets tougher than that, let me tell you. Now, back to work.'

He grinned at her then, and Michelle couldn't take her eyes of his mouth.

Damn him—when was he going to kiss her?!

~~~~~

Flick tried to get some sleep for almost an hour, but her head ached and eyes felt hot and itchy. She also felt guilty—she'd never had a single sick day while working for Leo, but he'd sent her home today even though there was nothing really wrong with her.

'Apart from a broken heart,' she reminded herself. But that shouldn't affect her performance at work. She was a professional. Nothing should stop her from performing to the best of her ability.

Flick rolled over onto her side and pressed her hot cheeks into the coolness of her pillow. Harrison's face flashed before her eyes, his eyes shining as he laughed at her. If she allowed herself to go there, she could imagine the taste and feel of his lips on hers. Flick made a low groaning sound in the back of the throat. She had to stop thinking like this! Harrison Lambert had walked away from her with barely a twitch. She was wasting energy wishing for something that was never going to happen.

A tap sounded on her bedroom door, and Michelle poked her head in.

'You have a visitor,' she said, her voice loaded with meaning.

Flick sat bolt upright in bed. 'Who?' she mouthed, her heart racing.

'Harrison,' Michelle mouthed back, waggling her eyebrows, a big smile on her face.

Flick swung her legs over the side of the bed, moved towards the door then glanced down at her crumpled work shirt and skirt. Michelle just shook her head impatiently.

'Like he cares,' she whispered, grabbing Flick's hand and pulling her out into the living room.

Harrison was standing looking out at the fire escape. She wondered if he was thinking of their night out there, of the secrets they shared, and the dreams they had dreamed together.

'Um, I'm just going for a walk,' Michelle said. 'There's heaps of cookies in the jar if you want them.'

Harrison turned to look at her as the door closed behind Michelle.

'Hi,' Flick said, daring a small smile. He wouldn't be here unless he couldn't stay away, would he?

'Are you okay? Leo said he sent you home sick,' he asked.

'Just a headache,' she said, waving a hand to show how unimportant it was.

'Did you take some aspirin?'

'Yes, doctor,' she said dutifully.

He flashed a brief smile at her, and she had to stop herself from walking across and kissing him.

'I came to tell you that I'm heading back to LA tomorrow. Leo's going to manage the rest of the renovation project,' he said suddenly.

Flick blinked. 'Are you coming back?' she asked.

He shook his head. Flick closed her eyes for a second.

'Is this because of what I told Marc?' she said. 'You don't have to worry, Harrison, I won't embarrass you around the hotel. I'm not going to stalk you or anything. I got the message.'

Harrison held her eye. 'I'm going because I love you, Flick,' he said.

'What?' she asked, confused and hurt and hopeful all at once.

'I told Marc how I feel,' he said.

He broke off and looked out over the fire escape again. Flick frowned. She was holding herself so tightly her back ached.

'What did he say?' she prompted.

'He wants me to choose—between him and you,' he said bluntly.

Flick gasped. Her hands curled into fists. 'He can't do that. Nobody can do that.'

Harrison shrugged. 'He has. He is.'

They stared at each other.

'I love you, Flick,' he said after a long silence.

'I love you, too. But that's not going to be enough, is it?' she asked.

Harrison ran a hand through his hair. 'I can't turn my back on my brother, Flick, any more than you could turn your back on your sister all those years ago.'

Flick flinched, hating that he was reminding her of before, of what had happened with Steph. But she could see the parallels, the dark irony that this was about two brothers, and once again she was going to be left broken-hearted and empty-handed. But so much more empty than last time. Infinitely more so.

'I think you should go now,' Flick said, biting her lip.

Harrison nodded once, tightly. Then he moved past her to the door and was gone. She moved to the sofa and watched out the window as he appeared in the street and crossed to his car. He glanced once back towards the building before sliding into the driver's seat. Flick closed her eyes for a moment, and when she opened them he was gone.

Harrison's jaw was set as he swiped his pass card in the lift and pressed the button for the penthouse. The floors flashed past and he flicked back the cuff on his shirt to check the time. He had a seven o'clock flight. Just enough time to pack and make arrangements for accommodation at the other end. Amanda was living in the LA house, and he'd given up his serviced apartment when he came east. 'There is always a Lassiter's hotel to stay in,' he thought wryly.

The thought of Amanda made him smile grimly. He'd thought that he would never feel worse than he had that day when he realised she'd made a laughing stock of their marriage. But he'd been so wrong. Sure, he'd been angry, and humiliated, and hurt. But he hadn't felt lost. He hadn't felt empty. He hadn't known that he was losing something beyond value.

But how he felt right now was irrelevant. He'd hurt Flick—that was the thing that was going to haunt him. It was one of life's little ironies that for the first time in his life he understood what true, unselfish love was, and he was walking away from it.

He let himself into the apartment and crossed to the bar. Then he frowned at the bottles of spirits lined up there. Nothing was going to make him feel any better, let alone a drink. Instead, he crossed to the window and stared out at the tiny people scurrying back and forth down below. Life went on, inevitably.

A door slammed somewhere in the suite, and Harrison turned around as Marc wandered out into the living area, a towel slung low around his waist. His hair was mussed, and Harrison frowned, checking his watch again. It was just after five. 'Another busy day at the office,' Harrison sarcastically thought.

Marc pulled up short when he saw him, his face shifting from relaxed to resentful to reserved in a flash of emotions.

'Thought you'd be gone by now,' he said.

'I got a later flight. I had things to sort out,' Harrison said.

'You went to Flick, didn't you?' Marc demanded.

'I wanted to explain why I was going. I wasn't going to just let her turn up at work tomorrow and hear I'd gone, for Pete's sake.'

Marc looked angry. 'I told you to choose.'

Harrison glared at his younger brother, his hurt too raw to allow for patience or understanding right now. 'You got what you wanted, Marc. Don't push it,' he said, his voice low and intense.

Marc shrugged. 'It was your choice, Harrison. You can still change your mind.'

'Marc, come on! Move it or lose it, pal. I'm due back on shift in twenty minutes, and you are not making me late again.'

Both Marc and Harrison turned towards the woman as she entered the living room, a white towel wrapped around her torso. Her step faltered when she saw Harrison, and she blushed to the roots of her blonde hair.

'Oh, hi, Mr Lambert,' she said.

'Sadie,' Harrison said tightly.

Sadie tugged at the hem of the towel, clearly feeling ill at ease. Marc avoided Harrison's eye, instead fussing with the towel around his own waist.

'Um, I can see that you guys were having a private conversation. I'll get out of your hair,' Sadie said as the tension thickened in the room.

She retreated, and Harrison turned towards his brother, waiting. After a long silence, Marc met his eye.

'Don't tell me, you're going to spout some archaic rule about not dipping my pen in the company ink,' Marc sneered.

'How long has this been going on?' Harrison asked coldly, a rock hard fury building inside him.

Marc shrugged, crossing to the bar and pulling a beer out of the hidden fridge.

'How long, Marc?'

'Does it matter?' he finally answered.

Harrison realised his hands were shaking he was so angry. 'All this time you've been spouting off about how much you love Flick, and you've been doing the housekeeping manager on the side. You're a real piece of work, Marc.'

'What difference does it make? Sadie knows the score, she knows this is just about fun. Flick is different. Flick is a keeper,' Marc said.

Harrison curled his hand into a fist. He and Marc had never been the sort of brothers who fought physically, but he had never faced this sort of provocation before.

'I nearly walked away from her because of you, Marc,' he said slowly. 'I almost trashed the best thing that's ever happened to me because you had me convinced that I'd stolen something that was yours.'

'You have, nothing's changed,' Marc said quickly.

'Bull. My God, I don't think you even know what love means,' Harrison said, striding towards the door.

'Where are you going?' Marc demanded.

'I'm going to apologise to Flick for choosing my spoilt brat of a brother over her.'

'Go on, then. But this is it, Harrison.'

'Fine. I know I'll sleep better at night,' Harrison bit back.

He pulled the door open, and Marc threw one last jibe after him.

'Congratulate Flick for me—she sure knows how to ruin people's lives,' Marc called.

Harrison paused in the doorway, then turned back to eye his brother coolly.

'You think Flick's to blame for all your problems, Marc? I see—now that you can't have the "one thing you've always wanted" it's all her fault.' Harrison took a couple of steps towards his brother, jabbing a hard finger at him. 'You made this mess, you and no one else. You asked Flick's sister to marry you, and you romanced Flick when you were committed to someone else. You were in a position to be a man about it, do the right thing. But you weren't up to that, were you? Don't go putting your weaknesses at Flick's door—she's worth ten of you. She came here alone, and she carved out a place for herself, and she stood up to all the prejudiced crap I threw at her because I bought the poison you and Chloe have been peddling all these years.'

Marc had gone pale beneath his tan.

'It's okay for you—everything has always been perfect for you. Great grades at school, top of your class at Harvard, marry the perfect girl, climb the company ladder—you get it all, Harrison. You never put a foot wrong. Do you have any idea how hard it is living in your shadow?' Marc said.

Harrison gave his brother a scathing head to toe. 'You need to grow up, Marc. Suck it up, and step up and take some responsibility. You don't want to be involved in the business? Say so, and find something else to do with your life. But do something, for Pete's sake. Because life moves on, no matter what you do, and if you're not careful, you're going to look back in ten years time and realise you've wasted the best part of your life.'

Harrison left him then, too angry to feel sorry for how lost his brother was. Maybe when some time had passed he might feel some sympathy for him—but right now all he had room for was hope that Flick would listen to a word he had to say after all the bulldust his family had put her through.

Flick stuffed her hands into her coat pockets and dropped her face down so that it was more protected by her scarf. It was snowing, and the crystal white flakes were catching on her eyelashes as she walked. The streetlights were already on, even though it was just after six. The rush hour was dying down, and the streets were reasonably quiet as people made their way home from work or out to dinner. Flick eyed a couple walking arm in arm, their heads so close the steam from their breath mingled in the air. Her mouth twisting, she turned away abruptly, stopping in front of a window display to avoid looking at someone else's love. She'd been walking for more than an hour, aimless, lost. Somehow it all felt a little more bearable if she kept moving.

Someone stopped beside her, another window shopper, and she shuffled to her right a little to give them some more room.

'I still think you'd look better in black,' the man said, and Flick realised it was Harrison standing next to her, coatless, the collar of his suit jacket turned up against the snow.

'I thought you were going,' she said stupidly. He shook his head, his eyes never leaving hers.

'I almost did. But then I found Marc in bed with Sadie from housekeeping, and I realised that I was the stupidest man on the planet to sacrifice loving you because my brother is terminally spoilt,' he said.

'So you're not going?' she asked, not quite daring to hope.

'No. I'm not going. I'm not going anywhere ever again, not without you,' he said.

Then he pulled her close and kissed her, and Flick went weak at the knees and had to lean against him in case she fell into a boneless mess on the pavement.

'I love you, Felicity Scully,' he said after a long, long time.

'I love you, Harrison Lambert,' she said.

A snowflake landed on his nose, and she realised that he was probably freezing in just his suit jacket.

'You must be cold,' she said, a slow warmth spreading inside her as she realised that this man standing within the circle of her arms was hers, and he loved her, and they were going to make things work.

'A little. But it's worth it,' he assured her.

Flick lowered her gaze for a moment then looked up at him, a cheeky glint in her eye. 'I think I should take you home and get you out of these wet clothes.'

'They're not wet,' he said automatically. 'Really, I'm fine.'

Flick nudged him with her elbow. 'Go with me on this. I think I should take you home and get you out of these wet clothes and into a nice warm bath.'

An arrested expression crossed Harrison's face. 'I see. Keep talking, this is starting to sound very interesting.'

He tucked her under his arm and turned her towards home.

'Have I ever told you what a great bathtub I have? A lethal weapon as a shower, sure, but as a bath, perfect. Big, deep. Plenty of room for two,' Flick said as they walked.

'Hmmm. Well, I guess we really should inspect it, since you'll be moving out soon.'

Flick stopped in her tracks. 'I will?'

'Oh yeah. I'm sure we can find somewhere

decent in Soho for you, me, and Michelle,' he said.

Flick felt a rush of tears well up in her eyes, and she blinked them away like crazy. It was too late, though, he'd seen them already. 'No tears, please, Ms Scully. We're celebrating, not commiserating.'

'I know. I love you,' she said, gazing up at him.

'I love you, too,' he said then he tagged her on the arm. 'Last one home gets the tap end of the bath.'

Before she realised what was happening, he'd taken off.

'Hey, no fair!' she called after him. Then she put her head down and started running him down.

Michelle knocked on Charlie's door juggling the bag of popcorn and the three videos. He answered the door wearing the low-slung, well-worn jeans she was beginning to have some serious romantic fantasies about.

'Sorry about this. But as soon as I heard the water running in the bathtub I knew there was definitely one too many people in that apartment,' Michelle said as she brushed past him and into his living area.

'It's cool. I was just getting sick of my book, anyway. What'd you bring?' he asked, pointing to her video selections.

'Horror, comedy and romance,' she said. She kept her eyes lowered, hoping he'd opt for romance.

'Comedy, every time,' he said. Michelle gritted her teeth and forced a smile.

'Comedy it is, then,' she said as lightly as she could.

Charlie grabbed a bowl from the kitchen and poured the popcorn into it.

'You know, I should really make you throw this stuff out. It's full of chemicals, and nowhere near as nice as fresh,' he said as he helped himself to a big handful.

'You got any fresh?' she asked, settling onto the couch and picking up the remote control.

'Nup.'

'Then shut up,' she said.

Charlie stuffed a piece of popcorn in her ear, and she swatted him off, laughing.

'Watch the movie, pest,' she said.

The credits rolled past, and Michelle tried to ignore her growing awareness of the tall male body stretched out next to hers. She risked a peek out of the corner of her eyes. His hair was a bit wet, like he'd just washed it. She frowned. He'd said he was reading a book, hadn't he?

He laughed, and she smelt the distinctive minty smell of toothpaste. So, he'd just showered and brushed his teeth. Michelle checked him out of the corner of her eye again. He looked relaxed, comfortable. Except that one leg was jiggling up and down, like he was nervous or something.

Suddenly she was gripped with a great sense of daring. Maybe because she'd just seen Flick race up the stairs with stars in her eyes, Harrison hot on her heels. Maybe because she hadn't thought about Connor much at all today. Instead, she'd been thinking of Charlie.

She turned to him, blurting out her question before she lost her courage. 'Charlie, do you think you're ever going to kiss me?' she asked.

He went very still then he shrugged one shoulder really casually.

'Don't know. You over that ex-boyfriend of yours yet?' he asked.

'Don't know. Maybe you should kiss me and find out,' Michelle suggested.

'Hmmm,' Charlie nodded, as though it was something he was going to have to give a great deal of thought to.

Michelle waited, but he still didn't do anything, just turned his eyes back to the movie and reached for another handful of popcorn.

Frustrated, she turned back to the movie. A few minutes ticked past, and slowly she got it. A big smile drew the corners of her mouth up. Turning on her knees, she leaned across and kissed him. His lips were firm and warm, and in an instant his hands were in her hair and he was pulling her close and kissing her like he couldn't get enough of her.

Just when her toes were curling in her shoes, he pulled back to look into her eyes.

'Have I ever told you you're beautiful Michelle Scully?' he asked.

'Nup. But don't let that stop you,' she said.

It seemed there was life after Connor O'Neill, after all, and that perhaps the Scully girls weren't so bad at this love thing when everything was said and done.

'Michelle?' Charlie murmured against her mouth.

'Yes?'

'Pay attention when I'm kissing you, please.'

'Sorry,' she said, and she closed her eyes and gave herself up to his kisses.

Neighbours®

Other Books In The Series:

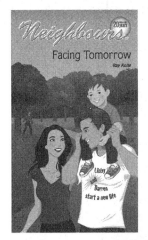